DATE DUE			

POEMS

NATHANIEL PARKER WILLIS.

GIRL LEADING HER BLIND MOTHER.   P. 286.

Front.

POEMS OF
NATHANIEL PARKER WILLIS

LONDON
GEO. ROUTLEDGE & SONS, Limited
BROADWAY, LUDGATE HILL

POEMS

OF

NATHANIEL PARKER WILLIS

WITH

A MEMOIR OF THE AUTHOR

AMS PRESS
NEW YORK

Reprinted from the edition of 1891, New York
First AMS EDITION published 1970
Manufactured in the United States of America

International Standard Book Number: 0-404-06989-4

Library of Congress Catalog Number: 70-128984

AMS PRESS INC.
NEW YORK, N.Y. 10003

MEMOIR

OF

NATHANIEL PARKER WILLIS.

———⋈———

THIS eminent author and distinguished journalist was born
in the town of Portland, in the State of Maine, on the 20th of
January 1807.   Unlike most persons who have created names
for themselves as men of genius, our author fortunately had
not to struggle against poverty; nor had he to acquire an
education by any unusual means.   On the contrary, his father,
who was at once a minister and an editor, was in a position
to give him the advantages of a first-class education.   At an
early period of his life he was sent to Yale College.   Here he
was noted as a diligent student, and early attracted attention.
He received a prize for Scriptural Poems, in 1828.   Even
before Mr. Willis left college, S. G. Goodrich, an eminent and
enterprising publisher of Boston (better known as the author
of "Peter Parley"), published his first book.   In college he
was best known as the writer of many pieces of poetry, pub-
lished under the signature of "Roy."   Like Pope, he "lisped
in numbers, for the numbers came."   But, unlike Pope, he
wrote almost as beautifully and faultlessly in his "lispings"

as at the latest period of his life. Willis was a principal writer
for the *Token*—one of the famous "Annuals" which were
exceedingly popular in those days. The *Token* was a mar-
vellously elegant appearing book, printed by Samuel N.
Dickenson, and illustrated by Cheney. Among its contributors
were such writers as Hawthorne, Mrs. Osgood, Pierpont,
Sprague, Mrs. Sigourney, and others whose names have since
become "household words" wherever "Milton's language is
the mother tongue." Mr. Willis was savagely attacked—
rather than criticised—in his youth. But these bitter de-
nunciations were evidently produced by envy at his successes,
for he was successful from the beginning. Indeed Mr. Good-
rich truly says of him, "that we have no other example of
literary success so early, so general, and so flattering." Mr.
Willis was a fine, tall, handsome man, with an intellectual face,
and refined manners. He also dressed with scrupulous care
and exquisite taste. He was, besides, gifted as a conversation-
alist. These qualities eminently fitted him to shine in society.
Doubtless many of his brother bards thought they were sacri-
ficing at the shrine of TRUTH, whilst they were hurling invec-
tives at his style, appearance, and manners. One of his
bitterest satirists was William J. Snelling—himself a scholar,
and a writer of great caustic power. It may be, perhaps, as
well to insert here a few of the savage lines that he addressed
to Mr. Willis, in the "New Year's Gift for Scribblers":—

> "Muse, shall we not a few brief lines afford
> To give poor Natty P. his due reward?
> What has he done to be despised of all,
> Within whose hands his harmless scribblings fall?"

It will be seen that Mr. Willis was gibbeted in "goodlie

companie "—and while Snelling is almost forgotten—('tis true, 'tis pity—pity 'tis, 'tis true)—the writers he so virulently assailed have floated triumphantly down the literary Ganges, with their burning lamps rendering the air bright and odorous to their many admirers.

Mr. Willis commenced his active literary life as a publisher very early. For we find him, in conjunction with Gen. George P. Morris, issuing the *New York Mirror*, in 1829. The next year he visited Europe, and soon the *Mirror* was enriched by his sprightly "Pencillings by the Way." Being an *attaché* of our legation at the French Court, he made the acquaintance of most of the men and women then rendering their country famous by their artistic and literary productions. He rambled through Greece and Turkey—then occupying the attention of all civilised people—and delighted readers by his brilliant sketches of persons and places seen on his journeyings. About this time he married a Miss Stace, daughter of a British General of that name. Having rather superciliously alluded to Captain Marryat in some of his writings, the author of "Peter Simple" challenged him—a bloodless duel ensued. He contributed many popular pieces to English magazines at this time, and Colburn, the London publishers, issued his "Inklings of Adventure," in several volumes. Returning to his native land in 1839, he retired to a beautiful country-seat on the Hudson—to which he gave the charming name of Glenmary. He also resumed his avocation as a publisher, issuing a paper called the *Corsair*—the name evidently suggested by Byron's hero of that title. Willis, although from his easy style, and apparently languid way of taking the world, had very few "Hours of Idleness;" for in addition to

his weekly " Letters from Under a Bridge," he contrived
to produce two plays, " Bianca Visconti" and "Tortesa the
Usurer,"—brimful of elegant writing.   In 1844 we find him
engaged with Gen. George P. Morris in editing the *Daily
Mirror.*   Here he became acquainted with the poet *Edgar
Allan Poe*—whose genius he greatly admired, and whose mis-
fortunes he sought to lessen.   Rendered low-spirited by the
death of his wife, he paid his second visit to Europe ; and as a
result, his " Dashes at Life with a Free Pencil " appeared in
1845.   The next year saw him again settled in New York, and
in the same year he married his second wife, a Miss Grinnel, of
a highly respectable Massachusetts family.   Parting with the
Mirror, our author, again in conjunction with Gen. George P.
Morris—the Castor and Pollux of the Press—began the pub-
lication of a weekly paper, *The Home Journal*—which became
a necessary adjunct to every refined drawing-room in the land.
Year after year saw new volumes of vivacious and elegant
prose appear, with his welcome name on their title-page.   But
in his latter years he suffered much from a species of decline
—to cure, or at least to alleviate which, he cruised through
the beautiful seas which lave the picturesque shores of the
West Indian Islands.   He has left some delightful word-
pictures of the ravishingly beautiful appearances of nature in
the tropics.   Losing his urbane and kindly partner, Morris, in
1864, Willis lived at his attractive highland home, Idlewild,
until the 21st day of January 1867, when he closed the eyes
which had seen so much and observed so truly.   As a *poet,*
Willis has produced many of the finest pieces with which our
literature is enriched ; as an essayest, he has scarcely a
superior ; as a traveller, he ranks with the first.   His style

both in prose and verses was eminently original, and peculiarly attractive, in that it had an indescribable, but charmingly perceptible grace about it, as delicate as the *bouquet* of the finest wines, or the odour of early violets. Mr. Willis' family all displayed more than usual literary ability. The famous *Ledger* author, *Fanny Fern*, wife of Parton the historian, was his sister; and Richard Storrs Willis, a musical composer and art critic, of fine reputation, is his brother.

CONTENTS.

—⋈—

COLLEGE POEMS—

CITY POEMS—

Mɪꜱᴄᴇʟʟᴀɴᴇᴏᴜꜱ Pᴏᴇᴍꜱ—

SCRIPTURAL POEMS.

SCRIPTURAL POEMS.

(FROM THE OLD TESTAMENT.)

———

HAGAR IN THE WILDERNESS.

(Genesis xxi.)

The morning broke.   Light stole upon the clouds
With a strange beauty.   Earth received again
Its garment of a thousand dyes; and leaves,
And delicate blossoms, and the painted flowers,
And everything that bendeth to the dew,
And stirreth with the daylight lifted up
Its beauty to the breath of that sweet morn.

   All things are dark to sorrow; and the light
And loveliness, and fragrant air were sad
To the dejected Hagar.   The moist earth
Was pouring odours from its spicy pores,
And the young birds were singing as if life
Were a new thing to them; but oh! it came
Upon her heart like discord, and she felt
How cruelly it tries a broken heart,
To see a mirth in any thing it loves.
She stood at Abraham's tent.   Her lips were press'd
Till the blood started; and the wandering veins

3

Of her transparent forehead were swelled out,
As if her pride would burst them.   Her dark eye
Was clear and tearless, and the light of heaven,
Which made its language legible, shot back,
From her long lashes, as it had been flame.
Her noble boy stood by her, with his hand
Clasp'd in her own, and his round, delicate feet,
Scarce train'd to balance on the tented floor,
Sandall'd for journeying.   He had look'd up
Into his mother's face until he caught
The spirit there, and his young heart was swelling
Beneath his dimpled bosom, and his form
Straighten'd up proudly in his tiny wrath,
As if his light proportions would have swell'd,
Had they but match'd his spirit, to the man.

Why bends the patriarch as he cometh now
Upon his staff so wearily? His beard
Is low upon his breast, and his high brow,
So written with the converse of his God,
Beareth the swollen vein of agony.
His lip is quivering, and his wonted step
Of vigour is not there; and, though the morn
Is passing fair and beautiful, he breathes
Its freshness as it were a pestilence.
Oh! man may bear with suffering: his heart
Is a strong thing, and godlike in the grasp
Of pain that wrings mortality; but tear
One chord affection clings to—part one tie
That binds him to a woman's delicate love—
And his great spirit yieldeth like a reed.

He gave to her the water and the bread,
But spoke no word, and trusted not himself
To look upon her face, but laid his hand

In silent blessing on the fair-hair'd boy,
And left her to her lot of loneliness.

Should Hagar weep？ May slighted woman turn,
And, as a vine the oak hath shaken off,
Bend lightly to her leaning trust again？
Oh no！ by all her loveliness—by all
That makes life poetry and beauty, no！
Make her a slave; steal from her rosy cheek
By needless jealousies; let the last star
Leave her a watcher by your couch of pain;
Wrong her by petulance, suspicion, all
That makes her cup a bitterness—yet give
One evidence of love, and earth has not
An emblem of devotedness like hers.
But oh！ estrange once—it boots not how—
By wrong or silence—anything that tells
A change has come upon your tenderness,—
And there is not a feeling out of heaven
Her pride o'ermastereth not.

She went her way with a strong step and slow—
Her press'd lip arch'd, and her clear eye undimm'd,
As if it were a diamond, and her form
Borne proudly up, as if her heart breathed through.
Her child kept on in silence, though she press'd
His hand till it was pain'd; for he had caught,
As I have said, her spirit, and the seed
Of a stern nation had been breathed upon.

The morning pass'd, and Asia's sun rode up
In the clear heaven, and every beam was heat.
The cattle of the hills were in the shade,
And the bright plumage of the Orient lay
On beating bosoms in her spicy trees.

It was an hour of rest ! but Hagar found
No shelter in the wilderness, and on
She kept her weary way, until the boy
Hung down his head, and open'd his parch'd lips
For water; but she could not give it him.
She laid him down beneath the sultry sky,—
For it was better than the close, hot breath
Of the thick pines,—and tried to comfort him ;
But he was sore athirst, and his blue eyes
Were dim and blood-shot, and he could not know
Why God denied him water in the wild.
She sat a little longer, and he grew
Ghastly and faint, as if he would have died.
It was too much for her.   She lifted him,
And bore him further on, and laid his head
Beneath the shadow of a desert shrub;
And, shrouding up her face, she went away,
And sat to watch, where he could see her not,
Till he should die; and, watching him, she mourn'd :—

"God stay thee in thine agony, my boy !
I cannot see thee die.   I cannot brook
        Upon thy brow to look,
And see death settle on my cradle joy.
How have I drunk the light of thy blue eye !
        And could I see thee die ?

"I did not dream of this when thou wast straying,
Like an unbound gazelle, among the flowers ;
        Or wiling the soft hours,
By the rich gush of water-sources playing,
Then sinking weary to thy smiling sleep,
        So beautiful and deep.

"Oh no! and when I watch'd by thee the while,
And saw thy bright lip curling in thy dream,
 And thought of the dark stream
In my own land of Egypt, the far Nile,
How pray'd I that my father's land might be
 An heritage for thee!

"And now the grave for its cold breast hath won thee!
And thy white delicate limbs the earth will press;
 And oh! my last caress
Must feel thee cold, for a chill hand is on thee.
How can I leave my boy, so pillow'd there
 Upon his clustering hair!"

She stood beside the well her God had given
To gush in that deep wilderness, and bathed
The forehead of her child until he laugh'd
In his reviving happiness, and lisp'd
His infant thought of gladness at the sight
Of the cool plashing of his mother's hand.

THE SACRIFICE OF ABRAHAM.

(GENESIS xxii.)

MORN breaketh in the east.   The purple clouds
Are putting on their gold and violet,
To look the meeter for the sun's bright coming.
Sleep is upon the waters and the wind ;
And nature, from the wavy forest-leaf
To her majestic master, sleeps.   As yet
There is no mist upon the deep blue sky,
And the clear dew is on the blushing bosoms
Of crimson roses in a holy rest.
How hallow'd is the hour of morning ! meet—
Ay, beautifully meet—for the pure prayer.
The patriarch standeth at his tented door,
With his white locks uncover'd.   'Tis his wont
To gaze upon that gorgeous Orient ;
And at that hour the awful majesty
Of man who talketh often with his God,
Is wont to come again, and clothe his brow
As at his fourscore strength.   But now, he seemeth
To be forgetful of his vigorous frame,
And boweth to his staff as at the hour
Of noontide sultriness.   And that bright sun—
He looketh at its pencill'd messengers,
Coming in golden raiment, as if all
Were but a graven scroll of fearfulness.
Ah, he is waiting till it herald in
The hour to sacrifice his much-loved son !

Light poureth on the world. And Sarah stands
Watching the steps of Abraham and her child
Along the dewy sides of the far hills,
And praying that her sunny boy faint not.
Would she have watch'd their path so silently,
If she had known that he was going up,
E'en in his fair-hair'd beauty, to be slain
As a white lamb for sacrifice ? They trod
Together onward, patriarch and child—
The bright sun throwing back the old man's shade
In straight and fair proportions, as of one
Whose years were freshly number'd. He stood up
Tall in his vigorous strength ; and, like a tree
Rooted in Lebanon, his frame bent not.
His thin white hairs had yielded to the wind,
And left his brow uncover'd ; and his face,
Impress'd with the stern majesty of grief
Nerved to a solemn duty, now stood forth
Like a rent rock, submissive, yet sublime.
But the young boy—he of the laughing eye
And ruby lip—the pride of life was on him.
He seem'd to drink the morning. Sun and dew,
And the aroma of the spicy trees,
And all that giveth the delicious East
Its fitness for an Eden, stole like light
Into his spirit, ravishing his thoughts
With love and beauty. Every thing he met,
Buoyant or beautiful, the lightest wing
Of bird or insect, or the palest dye
Of the fresh flowers, won him from his path ;
And joyously broke forth his tiny shout,
As he flung back his silken hair, and sprung
Away to some green spot or clustering vine,
To pluck his infant trophies. Every tree
And fragrant shrub was a new hiding-place ;

And he would crouch till the old man came by,
Then bound before him with his childish laugh,
Stealing a look behind him playfully,
To see if he had made his father smile.
The sun rode on in heaven.   The dew stole up
From the fresh daughters of the earth, and heat
Came like a sleep upon the delicate leaves,
And bent them with the blossoms to their dreams.
Still trod the patriarch on, with that same step,
Firm and unfaltering; turning not aside
To seek the olive shades, or lave their lips
In the sweet waters of the Syrian wells,
Whose gush hath so much music.   Weariness
Stole on the gentle boy, and he forgot
To toss his sunny hair from off his brow,
And spring for the fresh flowers and light wings
As in the early morning; but he kept
Close by his father's side, and bent his head
Upon his bosom like a drooping bud,
Lifting it not, save now and then to steal
A look up to the face whose sternness awed
His childishness to silence.

                              It was noon—
And Abraham on Moriah bow'd himself,
And buried up his face, and pray'd for strength.
He could not look upon his son, and pray;
But, with his hand upon the clustering curls
Of the fair, kneeling boy, he pray'd that God
Would nerve him for that hour.   Oh! man was made
For the stern conflict.   In a mother's love
There is more tenderness; the thousand chords,
Woven with every fibre of her heart,
Complain, like delicate harp-strings, at a breath;
But love in man is one deep principle,
Which, like a root grown in a rifted rock,

Abides the tempest. He rose up, and laid
The wood upon the altar. All was done.
He stood a moment—and a deep, quick flush
Pass'd o'er his countenance; and then he nerved
His spirit with a bitter strength, and spoke—
"Isaac! my only son!"—The boy look'd up,
And Abraham turn'd his face away, and wept.
"Where is the lamb, my father?"—Oh the tones,
The sweet, the thrilling music of a child!—
How it doth agonise at such an hour!—
It was the last deep struggle. Abraham held
His loved, his beautiful, his only son,
And lifted up his arm, and call'd on God—
And lo! God's angel stay'd him—and he fell
Upon his face, and wept.

THE SHUNAMMITE.

(2 KINGS viii.)

It was a sultry day of summer-time.
The sun pour'd down upon the ripen'd grain
With quivering heat, and the suspended leaves
Hung motionless. The cattle on the hills
Stood still, and the divided flock were all
Laying their nostrils to the cooling roots,
And the sky look'd like silver, and it seem'd
As if the air had fainted, and the pulse
Of nature had run down, and ceased to beat.

"Haste thee, my child!" the Syrian mother said,
"Thy father is athirst"—and, from the depths
Of the cool well under the leaning tree,
She drew refreshing water, and with thoughts
Of God's sweet goodness stirring at her heart,
She bless'd her beautiful boy, and to his way
Committed him.   And he went lightly on,
With his soft hands press'd closely to the cool
Stone vessel, and his little naked feet
Lifted with watchful care; and o'er the hills,
And through the light green hollows where the lambs
Go for the tender grass, he kept his way,
Wiling its distance with his simple thoughts,
Till, in the wilderness of sheaves, with brows
Throbbing with heat, he set his burden down.

Childhood is restless ever, and the boy
Stay'd not within the shadow of the tree,
But with a joyous industry went forth
Into the reaper's places, and bound up
His tiny sheaves, and plaited cunningly
The pliant withs out of the shining straw—
Cheering their labour on, till they forgot
The heat and weariness of their stooping toil
In the beguiling of his playful mirth.
Presently he was silent, and his eye
Closed as with dizzy pain; and with his hand
Press'd hard upon his forehead, and his breast
Heaving with the suppression of a cry,
He utter'd a faint murmur, and fell back
Upon the loosen'd sheaf, insensible.

They bore him to his mother, and he lay
Upon her knees till noon—and then he died !
She had watch'd every breath, and kept her hand
Soft on his forehead, and gazed in upon
The dreamy languor of his listless eye,
And she had laid back all his sunny curls
And kiss'd his delicate lip, and lifted him
Into her bosom, till her heart grew strong—
His beauty was so unlike death ! She lean'd
Over him now, that she might catch the low
Sweet music of his breath, that she had learn'd
To love when he was slumbering at her side
In his unconscious infancy—
                    —" So still !
'Tis a soft sleep ! How beautiful he lies,
With his fair forehead, and the rosy veins
Playing so freshly in his sunny cheek !
How could they say that he would die ! O God !
I could not lose him ! I have treasured all

His childhood in my heart, and even now,
As he has slept, my memory has been there,
Counting like treasures all his winning ways—
His unforgotten sweetness.—
          —"Yet so still!—
How like this breathless slumber is to death!
I could believe that in that bosom now
There were no pulse—it beats so languidly!
I cannot see it stir; but his red lip!
Death would not be so very beautiful!
And that half smile—would death have left *that* there?
—And should I not have felt that he would die?
And have I not wept over him?—and pray'd
Morning and night for him? and *could* he die?
—No—God will keep him! He will be my pride
Many long years to come, and his fair hair
Will darken like his father's, and his eye
Be of a deeper blue when he is grown;
And he will be so tall, and I shall look
With such a pride upon him!—*He* to die!"
And the fond mother lifted his soft curls,
And smiled, as if 'twere mockery to think
That such fair things could perish—
            —Suddenly
Her hand shrunk from him, and the colour fled
From her fix'd lip, and her supporting knees
Were shook beneath her child. Her hand had touch'd
His forehead, as she dallied with his hair—
And it was cold—like clay! Slow, very slow,
Came the misgiving that her child was dead.
She sat a moment, and her eyes were closed
In a dumb prayer for strength, and then she took
His little hand and press'd it earnestly—
And put her lip to his—and look'd again
Fearfully on him—and, then bending low,

She whisper'd in his ear, " My son !—my son ! "
And as the echo died, and not a sound
Broke on the stillness, and he lay there still—
Motionless on her knee—the truth *would* come !
And with a sharp, quick cry, as if her heart
Were crush'd, she lifted him and held him close
Into her bosom—with a mother's thought—
As if death had no power to touch him there !

.   .   .   .

The man of God came forth, and led the child
Unto his mother, and went on his way.
And he was there—her beautiful—her own—
Living and smiling on her—with his arms
Folded about her neck, and his warm breath
Breathing upon her lips, and in her ear
The music of his gentle voice once more !

JEPHTHAH'S DAUGHTER.

(JUDGES xi.)

SHE stood before her father's gorgeous tent,
To listen for his coming.   Her loose hair
Was resting on her shoulders, like a cloud
Floating around a statue, and the wind,
Just swaying her light robe, reveal'd a shape
Praxiteles might worship.   She had clasp'd
Her hands upon her bosom, and had raised
Her beautiful, dark, Jewish eyes to heaven,
Till the long lashes lay upon her brow.
Her lip was slightly parted, like the cleft
Of a pomegranate blossom ; and her neck,
Just where the cheek was melting to its curve
With the unearthly beauty sometimes there,
Was shaded, as if light had fallen off,
Its surface was so polish'd.   She was stilling
Her light, quick breath, to hear ; and the white rose
Scarce moved upon her bosom, as it swell'd,
Like nothing but a lovely wave of light,
To meet the arching of her queenly neck.
Her countenance was radiant with love.
She look'd like one to die for it—a being
Whose whole existence was the pouring out
Of rich and deep affections.   I have thought
A brother's and a sister's love were much ;
I know a brother's is—for I have been

A sister's idol—and I know how full
The heart may be of tenderness to her !
But the affection of a delicate child
For a fond father, gushing, as it does,
With the sweet springs of life, and pouring on,
Through all earth's changes, like a river's course—
Chasten'd with reverence, and made more pure
By the world's discipline of light and shade—
'Tis deeper—holier.

           The wind bore on
The leaden tramp of thousands. Clarion notes
Rang sharply on the ear at intervals ;
And the low, mingled din of mighty hosts
Returning from the battle, pour'd from far,
Like the deep murmur of a restless sea.
They came, as earthly conquerors always come,
With blood and splendour, revelry and woe.
The stately horse treads proudly—he hath trod
The brow of death, as well. The chariot-wheels
Of warriors roll magnificently on—
Their weight hath crush'd the fallen. *Man* is there—
Majestic, lordly man—with his sublime
And elevated brow, and godlike frame ;
Lifting his crest in triumph—for his heel
Hath trod the dying like a wine-press down !

The mighty Jephthah led his warriors on
Through Mizpeh's streets. His helm was proudly set,
And his stern lip curl'd slightly, as if praise
Were for the hero's scorn. His step was firm,
But free as India's leopard ; and his mail,
Whose shekels none in Israel might bear,
Was like a cedar's tassel on his frame.
His crest was Judah's kingliest ; and the look
Of his dark, lofty eye, and bended brow,

B

Might quell the lion. He led on; but thoughts
Seem'd gathering round which troubled him. The veins
Grew visible upon his swarthy brow,
And his proud lip was press'd as if with pain.
He trod less firmly; and his restless eye
Glanced forward frequently, as if some ill
He dared not meet were there. His home was near;
And men were thronging, with that strange delight
They have in human passions, to observe
The struggle of his feelings with his pride.
He gazed intensely forward. The tall firs
Before his tent were motionless. The leaves
Of the sweet aloe, and the clustering vines
Which half conceal'd his threshold, met his eye,
Unchanged and beautiful; and one by one,
The balsam, with its sweet-distilling stems,
And the Circassian rose, and all the crowd
Of silent and familiar things, stole up,
Like the recover'd passages of dreams.
He strode on rapidly. A moment more,
And he had reach'd his home; when lo! there sprang
One with a bounding footstep, and a brow
Of light, to meet him. Oh, how beautiful!—
Her dark eye flashing like a sun-lit gem—
And her luxuriant hair!—'twas like the sweep
Of a swift wing in visions. He stood still,
As if the sight had wither'd him. She threw
Her arms about his neck—he heeded not.
She call'd him "Father"—but he answer'd not.
She stood and gazed upon him. Was he wroth?
There was no anger in that blood-shot eye.
Had sickness seized him? She unclasp'd his helm,
And laid her white hand gently on his brow,
And the large veins felt stiff and hard, like cords.
The touch aroused him. He raised up his hands,

And spoke the name of God, in agony.
She knew that he was stricken, then; and rush'd
Again into his arms; and, with a flood
Of tears she could not bridle, sobb'd a prayer
That he would breathe his agony in words.
He told her—and a momentary flush
Shot o'er her countenance; and then the soul
Of Jephthah's daughter waken'd; and she stood
Calmly and nobly up, and said 'twas well—
And she would die. .   .   .   .   .

        The sun had well nigh set.
The fire was on the altar; and the priest
Of the high God was there.   A pallid man
Was stretching out his trembling hands to heaven,
As if he would have pray'd, but had no words—
And she who was to die, the calmest one
In Israel at that hour, stood up alone,
And waited for the sun to set.   Her face
Was pale, but very beautiful—her lip
Had a more delicate outline, and the tint
Was deeper; but her countenance was like
The majesty of angels.

        The sun set—
And she was dead—but not by violence.

DAVID'S GRIEF FOR HIS CHILD.

(2 Samuel xii.)

'Twas daybreak, and the fingers of the dawn
Drew the night's curtain, and touch'd silently
The eyelids of the king.   And David woke,
And robed himself, and pray'd.   The inmates, now,
Of the vast palace were astir, and feet
Glided along the tesselated floors
With a pervading murmur, and the fount
Whose music had been all the night unheard,
Play'd as if light had made it audible ;
And each one, waking, bless'd it unaware.
The fragrant strife of sunshine with the morn
Sweeten'd the air to ecstasy ! and now
The king's wont was to lie upon his couch
Beneath the sky-roof of the inner court,
And, shut in from the world, but not from heaven,
Play with his loved son by the fountain's lip ;
For, with idolatry confess'd alone
To the rapt wires of his reproofless harp,
He loved the child of Bathsheba.   And when
The golden selvedge of his robe was heard
Sweeping the marble pavement, from within
Broke forth a child's laugh suddenly, and words—
Articulate, perhaps, to *his* heart only—
Pleading to come to him.   They brought the boy—
An infant cherub, leaping as if used

To hover with that motion upon wings,
And marvellously beautiful!   His brow
Had the inspired up-lift of the king's,
And kingly was his infantine regard;
But his ripe mouth was of the ravishing mould
Of Bathsheba's—the hue and type of love,
Rosy and passionate—and oh! the moist
Unfathomable blue of his large eyes
Gave out its light as twilight shows a star,
And drew the heart of the beholder in!—
And this was like his mother.

               David's lips
Moved with unutter'd blessings, and awhile
He closed the lids upon his moisten'd eyes,
And, with the round cheek of the nestling boy
Press'd to his bosom, sat as if afraid
That but the lifting of his lids might jar
His heart's cup from its fulness.   Unobserved,
A servant of the outer court had knelt
Waiting before him; and a cloud the while
Had rapidly spread o'er the summer heaven;
And, as the chill of the withdrawing sun
Fell on the king, he lifted up his eyes
And frown'd upon the servant—for that hour
Was hallow'd to his heart and his fair child,
And none might seek him.   And the king arose,
And with a troubled countenance look'd up
To the fast-gathering darkness; and, behold,
The servant bow'd himself to earth, and said,
"Nathan the prophet cometh from the Lord!"
And David's lips grew white, and with a clasp
Which wrung a murmur from the frighted child,
He drew him to his breast, and cover'd him
With the long foldings of his robe, and said,
"I will come forth.   Go now!"   And lingeringly,

With kisses on the fair uplifted brow,
And mingled words of tenderness and prayer
Breaking in tremulous accents from his lips,
He gave them the child, and bow'd his head
Upon his breast with agony.   And so,
To hear the errand of the man of God,
He fearfully went forth.

.   .   .   .   .   .

It was the morning of the seventh day.
A hush was in the palace, for all eyes
Had woke before the morn; and they who drew
The curtains to let in the welcome light,
Moved in their chambers with unslipper'd feet,
And listen'd breathlessly.   And still no stir !
The servants who kept watch without the door
Sat motionless; the purple casement-shades
From the low windows had been rolled away,
To give the child air; and the flickering light
That all the night, within the spacious court,
Had drawn the watcher's eyes to one spot only,
Paled with the sunrise and fled in.

                              And hush'd
With more than stillness was the room where lay
The king's son on his mother's breast.   His locks
Slept at the lips of Bathsheba unstirr'd—
So fearfully, with heart and pulse kept down,
She watch'd his breathless slumber.   The low moan
That from his lips all night broke fitfully
Had silenced with the daybreak, and a smile
Play'd in his parted mouth ; and though his lids
Hid not the blue of his unconscious eyes,
His senses seem'd all peacefully asleep,
And Bathsheba in silence bless'd the morn
That brought back hope to her !   But when the king
Heard not the voice of the complaining child,

Nor breath from out the room, nor foot astir—
But morning there—so welcomeless and still—
He groan'd and turned upon his face. The nights
Had wasted, and the mornings come, and days
Crept through the sky, unnumber'd by the king,
Since the child sicken'd ; and, without the door,
Upon the bare earth prostrate, he had lain—
Listening only to the moans that brought
Their inarticulate tidings, and the voice
Of Bathsheba, whose pity and caress,
In loving utterance all broke with tears,
Spoke as his heart would speak if he were there,
And fill'd his prayer with agony.   O God !
To Thy bright mercy-seat the way is far !
How fail the weak words while the heart keeps on !
And when the spirit, mournfully, at last,
Kneels at Thy throne, how cold, how distantly
The comforting of friends falls on the ear—
The anguish they would speak to, gone to Thee !

But suddenly the watchers at the door
Rose up, and they who minister'd within
Crept to the threshold and look'd earnestly
Where the king lay.   And still, while Bathsheba
Held the unmoving child upon her knees,
The curtains were let down, and all came forth,
And, gathering with fearful looks apart,
Whisper'd together.
    And the king arose,
And gazed on them a moment, and with voice
Of quick, uncertain utterance, he ask'd,
" Is the child dead ? "   They answered, " He is dead ! "
But when they look'd to see him fall again
Upon his face, and rend himself and weep —
For, while the child was sick, his agony

Would bear no comforters, and they had thought
His heartstrings with the tidings must give way—
Behold ! his face grew calm, and, with his robe
Gather'd together like his kingly wont,
He silently went in.

    And David came,
Robed and anointed, forth, and to the house
Of God went up to pray.   And he return'd,
And they set bread before him, and he ate—
And when they marvell'd, said, " *Wherefore mourn ?*
The child is dead, and I shall go to him—
But he will not return to me."

ABSALOM.

(2 SAMUEL xix.)

THE waters slept. Night's silvery veil hung low
On Jordan's bosom, and the eddies curl'd
Their glassy rings beneath it, like the still,
Unbroken beating of the sleeper's pulse.
The reeds bent down the stream the willow leaves,
With a soft cheek upon the lulling tide,
Forgot the lifting winds; and the long stems,
Whose flowers the water, like a gentle nurse,
Bears on its bosom, quietly gave way,
And lean'd in graceful attitudes, to rest.
How strikingly the course of nature tells,
By its light heed of human suffering,
That it was fashion'd for a happier world!
   King David's limbs were weary. He had fled
From far Jerusalem; and now he stood,
With his faint people, for a little rest
Upon the shore of Jordan.   The light wind
Of morn was stirring, and he bared his brow
To its refreshing breath; for he had worn
The mourner's covering, and he had not felt
That he could see his people until now.
They gather'd round him on the fresh green bank,
And spoke their kindly words; and, as the sun
Rose up in heaven, he knelt among them there,
And bow'd his head upon his hands to pray.

Oh ! when the heart is full—when bitter thoughts
Come crowding thickly up for utterance,
And the poor common words of courtesy
Are such a very mockery—how much
The bursting heart may pour itself in prayer !
He pray'd for Israel—and his voice went up
Strongly and fervently.   He pray'd for those
Whose love had been his shield—and his deep tones
Grew tremulous.   But, oh ! for Absalom—
For his estranged, misguided Absalom—
The proud, bright being, who had burst away
In all his princely beauty, to defy
The heart that cherish'd him—for him he pour'd,
In agony that would not be controll'd,
Strong supplication ; and forgave him there,
Before his God, for his deep sinfulness.

   .   .   .   .   .

    The pall was settled.   He who slept beneath
Was straighten'd for the grave ; and, as the folds
Sunk to the still proportions, they betray'd
The matchless symmetry of Absalom.
His hair was yet unshorn, and silken curls
Were floating round the tassels as they sway'd
To the admitted air, as glossy now
As when, in hours of gentle dalliance, bathing
The snowy fingers of Judea's daughters.
His helm was at his feet : his banner, soil'd
With trailing through Jerusalem, was laid,
Reversed, beside him : and the jewell'd hilt,
Whose diamonds lit the passage of his blade,
Rested, like mockery, on his cover'd brow.
The soldiers of the king trod to and fro,
Clad in the garb of battle ; and their chief,
The mighty Joab, stood beside the bier,
And gazed upon the dark pall steadfastly,

As if he fear'd the slumberer might stir.
A slow step startled him.   He grasp'd his blade
As if a trumpet rang ; but the bent form
Of David enter'd, and he gave command,
In a low tone, to his few followers,
And left him with his dead.   The king stood still
Till the last echo died ; then, throwing off
The sackcloth from his brow, and laying back
The pall from the still features of his child,
He bow'd his head upon him, and broke forth
In the resistless eloquence of woe :

" Alas ! my noble boy ! that thou shouldst die !
    Thou, who wert made so beautifully fair !
That death should settle in thy glorious eye,
    And leave his stillness in this clustering hair !
How could he mark thee for the silent tomb !
        My proud boy, Absalom !

" Cold is thy brow, my son ! and I am chill,
    As to my bosom I have tried to press thee !
How was I wont to feel my pulses thrill,
    Like a rich harp-string yearning to caress thee,
And hear thy sweet ' *My father !* ' from these dumb
        And cold lips, Absalom !

" But death is on thee.   I shall hear the gush
    Of music, and the voices of the young ;
And life will pass me in the mantling blush,
    And the dark tresses to the soft winds flung ;—
But thou no more, with thy sweet voice, shalt come
        To meet me, Absalom !

" And oh ! when I am stricken, and my heart,
    Like a bruised reed, is waiting to be broken,

How will its love for thee, as I depart,
   Yearn for thine ear to drink its last deep token !
It were so sweet, amid death's gathering gloom,
     To see thee, Absalom !

" And now, farewell ! 'Tis hard to give thee up,
   With death so like a gentle slumber on thee ;—
And thy dark sin !—Oh ! I could drink the cup,
   If from this woe its bitterness had won thee.
May God have call'd thee, like a wanderer, home,
     My lost boy, Absalom ! "

He cover'd up his face, and bow'd himself
A moment on his child : then, giving him
A look of melting tenderness, he clasp'd
His hands convulsively, as if in prayer ;
And, as if strength were given him of God,
He rose up calmly, and composed the pall
Firmly and decently—and left him there—
As if his rest had been a breathing sleep.

RIZPAH WITH HER SONS.

(The day before they were hanged on Gibeah.)

(2 SAMUEL xxi.)

" BREAD for my mother !" said the voice of one
Darkening the door of Rizpah. She look'd up—
And lo ! the princely countenance and mien
Of dark-brow'd Armoni. The eye of Saul—
The very voice and presence of the king—
Limb, port, and majesty,—were present there,
Mock'd like an apparition in her son.
Yet, as he stoop'd his forehead to her hand
With a kind smile, a something of his mother
Unbent the haughty arching of his lip,
And, through the darkness of the widow's heart
Trembled a nerve of tenderness that shook
Her thought of pride all suddenly to tears.

" Whence comest thou ?" said Rizpah.

                         " From the house
Of David. In his gate there stood a soldier—
This in his hand. I pluck'd it, and I said,
' *A king's son takes it for his hungry mother !* '
God stay the famine !"
.   .   .   .   .   As he spoke, a step,
Light as an antelope's, the threshold press'd,
And like a beam of light into the room

Enter'd Mephibosheth.   What bird of heaven
Or creature of the wild—what flower of earth—
Was like this fairest of the sons of Saul?
The violet's cup was harsh to his blue eye.
Less agile was the fierce barb's fiery step.
His voice drew hearts to him.   His smile was like
The incarnation of some blessed dream—
Its joyousness so sunn'd the gazer's eye!
Fair were his locks.   His snowy teeth divided
A bow of Love, drawn with a scarlet thread.
His cheek was like the moist heart of the rose;
And, but for nostrils of that breathing fire
That turns the lion back, and limbs as lithe
As is the velvet muscle of the pard,
Mephibosheth had been too fair for man.

As if he were a vision that would fade,
Rizpah gazed on him.   Never, to her eye,
Grew his bright form familiar, but, like stars,
That seem'd each night new lit in a ... heaven,
He was each morn's sweet gift to her.   She loved
Her firstborn, as a mother loves her child,
Tenderly, fondly.   But for him—the last—
What had she done for heaven to be his mother?
Her heart rose in her throat to hear his voice;
She look'd at him for ever through her tears;
Her utterance, when she spoke to him, sank down,
As if the lightest thought of him had lain
In an unfathom'd cavern of her soul.
The morning light was part of him, to her—
What broke the day for, but to show his beauty?
The hours but measured time till he should come;
Too tardy sang the bird when he was gone;
She would have shut the flowers—and call'd the star
Back to the mountain top—and bade the sun

Pause at eve's golden door—to wait for him !
Was this a heart gone wild ?—or is the love
Of mothers like a madness ?—Such as this
Is many a poor one in her humble home,
Who silently and sweetly sits alone,
Pouring her life all out upon her child.
What cares she that he does not feel how close
Her heart beats after his—that all unseen
Are the fond thoughts that follow him by day,
And watch his sleep like angels ?   And, when moved
By some sore needed Providence, he stops
In his wild path and lifts a thought to heaven,
What cares the mother that he does not see
The link between the blessing and her prayer ?

He who once wept with Mary—angels keeping
Their unthank'd watch—are a foreshadowing
Of what love is in heaven.   We may believe
That we shall know each other's forms hereafter,
And, in the bright fields of the better land,
Call the lost dead to us.   Oh, conscious heart !
That in the lone paths of this shadowy world
Hast bless'd all light, however dimly shining,
That broke upon the darkness of thy way—
Number thy lamps of love, and tell me, now,
How many canst thou relight at the stars
And blush not at their burning ?   One—one only,
Lit while your pulses by one heart kept time,
And fed with faithful fondness to your grave—
(Tho' sometimes with a hand stretch'd back from heaven,)
Steadfast thro' all things—near, when most forgot—
And with its finger of unerring truth
Pointing the lost way in thy darkest hour—
One lamp—*thy mother's love*—amid the stars
Shall lift its pure flame changeless, and, before

The throne of God, burn through eternity—
Holy—as it was lit and lent thee here.

The hand in salutation gently raised
To the bow'd forehead of the princely boy,
Linger'd amid his locks.   " I sold," he said
" My Lybian barb for but a cake of meal—
Lo ! this—my mother !   As I pass'd the street,
I hid it in my mantle, for there stand
Famishing mothers, with their starving babes,
At every threshold ; and wild, desperate men
Prowl, with the eyes of tigers, up and down,
Watching to rob those who, from house to house,
Beg for the dying.   Fear not thou, my mother !
Thy sons will be Elijah's ravens to thee ! "

[UNFINISHED.]

SCRIPTURAL POEMS.

(FROM THE NEW TESTAMENT.)

BAPTISM OF CHRIST.

(St. Matthew iii.)

It was a green spot in the wilderness,
Touch'd by the River Jordan. The dark pine
Never had dropp'd its tassels on the moss
Tufting the leaning bank, nor on the grass
Of the broad circle stretching evenly
To the straight larches, had a heavier foot
Than the wild heron's trodden. Softly in
Through a long aisle of willows, dim and cool,
Stole the clear waters with their muffled feet,
And, hushing as they spread into the light,
Circled the edges of the pebbled tank
Slowly, then rippled through the woods away.
Hither had come th' Apostle of the wild,
Winding the river's course. 'Twas near the flush
Of eve, and, with a multitude around,
Who from the cities had come out to hear,
He stood breast-high amid the running stream,
Baptizing as the Spirit gave him power.
His simple raiment was of camel's hair,
A leathern girdle close about his loins,

His beard unshorn, and for his daily meat
The locust and wild honey of the wood—
But like the face of Moses on the Mount
Shone his rapt countenance, and in his eye
Burn'd the mild fire of love—and as he spoke
The ear lean'd to him, and persuasion swift
To the chain'd spirit of the listener stole.

Silent upon the green and sloping bank
The people sat, and while the leaves were shook
With the birds dropping early to their nests,
And the grey eve came on, within their hearts
They mused if he were Christ. The rippling stream
Still turn'd its silver courses from his breast
As he divined their thought. "I but baptize,"
He said, "with water; but there cometh One,
The lachet of Whose shoes I may not dare
E'en to unloose. He will baptize with fire
And with the Holy Ghost." And lo! while yet
The words were on his lips, he raised his eyes,
And on the bank stood Jesus. He had laid
His raiment off, and with His loins alone
Girt with a mantle, and His perfect limbs,
In their angelic slightness, meek and bare,
He waited to go in. But John forbade,
And hurried to His feet and stayed Him there,
And said, "Nay, Master! I have need of *Thine*,
Not Thou of *mine!*" And Jesus, with a smile
Of heavenly sadness, met his earnest looks,
And answer'd, "Suffer it to be so now;
For thus it doth become Me to fulfil
All righteousness." And, leaning to the stream,
He took around him the Apostle's arm,
And drew him gently to the midst. The wood
Was thick with the dim twilight as they came

Up from the water.   With his clasped hands
Laid on his breast, th' Apostle silently
Follow'd his Master's steps—when lo ! a light,
Bright as the tenfold glory of the sun,
Yet lambent as the softly burning stars,
Envelop'd them, and from the heavens away
Parted the dim blue ether like a veil ;
And as a voice, fearful exceedingly,
Broke from the midst, "THIS IS MY MUCH-LOVED SON,
IN WHOM I AM WELL PLEASED," a snow-white dove,
Floating upon its wings, descended through,
And shedding a swift music from its plumes,
Circled, and flutter'd to the Saviour's breast.

CHRIST'S ENTRANCE INTO JERUSALEM.

(ST. MATTHEW xi.)

HE sat upon the " ass's foal " and rode
Toward Jerusalem.   Beside Him walk'd,
Closely and silently, the faithful Twelve,
And on before Him went a multitude
Shouting Hosannas, and with eager hands
Strewing their garments thickly in His way.
Th' unbroken foal beneath Him gently stepp'd,
Tame as its patient dam ; and as the song
Of " Welcome to the Son of David " burst
Forth from a thousand children, and the leaves
Of the waved branches touch'd its silken ears,
It turn'd its wild eye for a moment back,
And then, subdued by an invisible hand,
Meekly trode onward with its slender feet.

The dew's last sparkle from the grass had gone
As He rode up Mount Olivet. The woods
Threw their cool shadows freshly to the west,
And the light foal, with quick and toiling step,
And head bent low, kept its unslacken'd way
Till its soft mane was lifted by the wind
Sent o'er the Mount from Jordan. As He reach'd
The summit's breezy pitch, the Saviour raised
His calm blue eye—there stood Jerusalem !
Eagerly He bent forward, and beneath
His mantle's passive folds, a bolder line
Than the wont slightness of His perfect limbs
Betray'd the swelling fulness of His heart.
There stood Jerusalem ! How fair she look'd—
The silver sun on all her palaces,
And her fair daughters 'mid the golden spires
Tending their terrace flowers, and Kedron's stream
Lacing the meadows with its silver band,
And wreathing its mist-mantle on the sky
With the morn's exhalations. There she stood—
Jerusalem—the city of His love,
Chosen from all the earth ; Jerusalem—
That knew Him not—and had rejected Him ;
Jerusalem—for whom He came to die !
The shouts redoubled from a thousand lips
At the fair sight ; the children leap'd and sang
Louder Hosannas ; the clear air was fill'd
With odour from the trampled olive-leaves—
But "Jesus wept." The loved disciple saw
His Master's tears, and closer to His side
He came with yearning looks ; and on his neck
The Saviour leant with heavenly tenderness,
And mourn'd—"How oft, Jerusalem ! would I
Have gather'd you, as gathereth a hen
Her brood beneath her wings—but ye would not !"

He thought not of the death that He should die—
He thought not of the thorns He knew must pierce
His forehead—of the buffet on the cheek—
The scourge, the mocking homage, the foul scorn !—
Gethsemane stood out beneath His eye
Clear in the morning sun, and there, He knew,
While they who " could not watch with Him one hour "
Were sleeping, He should sweat great drops of blood,
Praying the " cup might pass." And Golgotha
Stood bare and desert by the city wall,
And in its midst, to His prophetic eye,
Rose the rough cross, and its keen agonies
Were number'd all—the nails were in His feet—
Th' insulting sponge was pressing on His lips—
The blood and water gushing from His side—
The dizzy faintness swimming in His brain—
And, while His own disciples fled in fear,
A world's death-agonies all mix'd in His !
Ay !—He forgot all this. He only saw
Jerusalem,—the chos'n—the loved—the lost !
He only felt that for her sake His life
Was vainly giv'n ; and, in His pitying love,
The sufferings that would clothe the heavens in black
Were quite forgotten. Was there ever love,
In earth or heaven, equal unto this ?

THE HEALING OF THE DAUGHTER OF JAIRUS.

(St. Mark v.)

FRESHLY the cool breath of the coming eve
Stole through the lattice, and the dying girl
Felt it upon her forehead. She had lain
Since the hot noontide in a breathless trance—
Her thin pale fingers clasp'd within the hand
Of the heart-broken Ruler, and her breast,
Like the dead marble, white and motionless.
The shadow of a leaf lay on her lips,
And, as it stirr'd with the awakening wind,
The dark lids lifted from her languid eyes,
And her slight fingers moved, and heavily
She turned upon her pillow. He was there—
The same loved, tireless watcher, and she look'd
Into his face until her sight grew dim
With the fast-falling tears; and, with a sigh
Of tremulous weakness murmuring his name,
She gently drew his hand upon her lips,
And kiss'd it as she wept. The old man sunk
Upon his knees, and in the drapery
Of the rich curtains buried up his face;
And when the twilight fell, the silken folds
Stirr'd with his prayer, but the slight hand he held
Had ceased its pressure—and he could not hear,
In the dead utter silence, that a breath
Came through her nostrils—and her temples gave
To his nice touch no pulse—and at her mouth
He held the lightest curl that on her neck

Lay with a mocking beauty, and his gaze
Ached with its deathly stillness.

. . . .

      It was night—
And softly o'er the Sea of Galilee
Danced the breeze-ridden ripples to the shore,
Tipp'd with the silver sparkles of the moon.
The breaking waves play'd low upon the beach
Their constant music, but the air beside
Was still as starlight, and the Saviour's voice,
In its rich cadences unearthly sweet,
Seem'd like some just-born harmony in the air,
Waked by the power of wisdom.   On a rock,
With the broad moonlight falling on His brow,
He stood and taught the people.   At His feet
Lay His small scrip, and pilgrim's scallop-shell,
And staff—for they had waited by the sea
Till He came o'er from Gadarene, and pray'd
For His wont teachings as He came to land.
His hair was parted meekly on His brow,
And the long curls from off His shoulders fell,
As He leaned forward earnestly, and still
The same calm cadence, passionless and deep—
And in His looks the same mild majesty—
And in His mien the sadness mix'd with power—
Fill'd them with love and wonder.   Suddenly,
As on His words entrancedly they hung,
The crowd divided, and among them stood
JAIRUS THE RULER.   With his flowing robe
Gather'd in haste about his loins, he came,
And fix'd his eyes on Jesus.   Closer drew
The twelve disciples to their Master's side ;
And silently the people shrunk away,
And left the haughty Ruler in the midst
Alone.   A moment longer on the face

Of the meek Nazarene he kept his gaze,
And, as the Twelve looked on him, by the light
Of the clear moon they saw a glistening tear
Steal to his silver beard; and, drawing nigh
Unto the Saviour's feet, he took the hem
Of His coarse mantle, and with trembling hands
Press'd it upon his lips, and murmur'd low,
" *Master! my daughter!* "

  .   .   .   .

              The same silvery light
That shone upon the lone rock by the sea
Slept on the Ruler's lofty capitals,
As at the door he stood, and welcomed in
Jesus and His disciples.   All was still.
The echoing vestibule gave back the slide
Of their loose sandals, and the arrowy beam
Of moonlight, slanting to the marble floor,
Lay like a spell of silence in the rooms,
As Jairus led them on.   With hushing steps
He trod the winding stair; but ere he touch'd
The latchet, from within a whisper came,
" *Trouble the Master not—for she is dead!* "
And his faint hand fell nerveless at his side,
And his steps falter'd, and his broken voice
Choked in its utterance;—but a gentle hand
Was laid upon his arm, and in his ear
The Saviour's voice sank thrillingly and low,
" *She is not dead—but sleepeth.* "

                  They pass'd in.
The spice-lamps in the alabaster urns
Burn'd dimly, and the white and fragrant smoke
Curl'd indolently on the chamber walls.
The silken curtains slumber'd in their folds—
Not even a tassel stirring in the air—
And as the Saviour stood beside the bed,

And pray'd inaudibly, the Ruler heard
The quickening division of His breath
As He grew earnest inwardly.   There came
A gradual brightness o'er His calm, sad face ;
And, drawing nearer to the bed, He moved
The silken curtains silently apart,
And look'd upon the maiden.

       Like a form
Of matchless sculpture in her sleep she lay—
The linen vesture folded on her breast,
And over it her white transparent hands,
The blood still rosy in their tapering nails.
A line of pearl ran through her parted lips,
And in her nostrils, spiritually thin,
The breathing curve was mockingly like life ;
And round beneath the faintly tinted skin
Ran the light branches of the azure veins ;
And on her cheek the jet lash overlay,
Matching the arches pencill'd on her brow.
Her hair had been unbound, and falling loose
Upon her pillow, hid her small round ears
In curls of glossy blackness, and about
Her polish'd neck, scarce touching it, they hung,
Like airy shadows floating as they slept.
'Twas heavenly beautiful.   The Saviour raised
Her hand from off her bosom, and spread out
The snowy fingers in His palm, and said,
" *Maiden ! Arise !* "—and suddenly a flush
Shot o'er her forehead, and along her lips
And through her cheek the rallied colour ran ;
And the still outline of her graceful form
Stirr'd in the linen vesture ; and she clasp'd
The Saviour's hand, and fixing her dark eyes
Full on His beaming countenance—AROSE !

THE WIDOW OF NAIN.

(St. Luke vii. 11.)

The Roman sentinel stood, helm'd and tall,
Beside the gate of Nain.   The busy tread
Of comers to the city mart was done,
For it was almost noon, and a dead heat
Quiver'd upon the fine and sleeping dust,
And the cold snake crept panting from the wall,
And bask'd his scaly circles in the sun.
Upon his spear the soldier lean'd, and kept
His idle watch, and, as his drowsy dream
Was broken by the solitary foot
Of some poor mendicant, he raised his head
To curse him for a tributary Jew,
And slumberously dozed on.

        'Twas now high noon.
The dull, low murmur of a funeral
Went through the city—the sad sound of feet
Unmix'd with voices—and the sentinel
Shook off his slumber, and gazed earnestly
Up the wide street along whose paved way
The silent throng crept slowly.   They came on,
Bearing a body heavily on its bier,
And by the crowd that in the burning sun
Walk'd with forgetful sadness, 'twas of one
Mourn'd with uncommon sorrow.   The broad gate
Swung on its hinges, and the Roman bent
His spear-point downwards as the bearers pass'd,
Bending beneath their burden.   There was one—
Only one mourner.   Close behind the bier,

Crumpling the pall up in her wither'd hands,
Follow'd an aged woman. Her short steps
Falter'd with weakness, and a broken moan
Fell from her lips, thicken'd convulsively
As her heart bled afresh. The pitying crowd
Follow'd apart, but no one spoke to her.
She had no kinsmen. She had lived alone—
A widow with one son. He was her all—
The only tie she had in the wide world—
And he was dead. They could not comfort her.

Jesus drew near to Nain as from the gate
The funeral came forth. His lips were pale
With the noon's sultry heat. The beaded sweat
Stood thickly on His brow, and on the worn
And simple latchets of His sandals lay
Thick the white dust of travel. He had come
Since sunrise from Capernaum, staying not
To wet His lips by green Bethsaida's pool,
Nor wash His feet in Kishon's silver springs,
Nor turn Him southward upon Tabor's side
To catch Gilboa's light and spicy breeze.
Genesareth stood cool upon the east,
Fast by the Sea of Galilee, and there
The weary traveller might bide till eve,
And on the alders of Bethulia's plains
The grapes of Palestine hung ripe and wild ;
Yet turn'd He not aside, but, gazing on,
From every swelling mount, He saw afar,
Amid the hills, the humble spires of Nain,
The place of His next errand ; and the path
Touch'd not Bethulia, and a league away
Upon the east lay pleasant Galilee.

Forth from the city gate the pitying crowd
Follow'd the stricken mourner. They came near

The place of burial, and, with straining hands,
Closer upon her breast she clasp'd the pall,
And with a gasping sob, quick as a child's,
And an inquiring wildness flashing through
The thin grey lashes of her fever'd eyes,
She came where Jesus stood beside the way.
He look'd upon her, and His heart was moved.
" Weep not ! " He said ; and as they stay'd the bier,
And at His bidding laid it at His feet,
He gently drew the pall from out her grasp,
And laid it back in silence from the dead.
With troubled wonder the mute throng drew near,
And gazed on His calm looks.   A minute's space
He stood and pray'd.   Then, taking the cold hand,
He said, " Arise ! "   And instantly the breast
Heaved in its cerements, and a sudden flush
Ran through the lines of the divided lips,
And, with a murmur of his mother's name,
He trembled and sat upright in his shroud.
And, while the mourner hung upon his neck,
Jesus went calmly on His way to Nain.

THE LEPER.
(St. Luke xvii.)

" Room for the leper ! room ! "   And, as he came,
The cry pass'd on—" Room for the leper ! room ! "
Sunrise was slanting on the city gates
Rosy and beautiful, and from the hills
The early risen poor were coming in,
Duly and cheerfully to their toil, and up
Rose the sharp hammer's clink, and the far hum

Of moving wheels and multitudes astir,
And all that in a city murmur swells—
Unheard but by the watcher's weary ear,
Aching with night's dull silence, or the sick
Hailing the welcome light and sounds that chase
The death-like images of the dark away.
" Room for the leper ! " And aside they stood—
Matron, and child, and pitiless manhood—all
Who met him on his way—and let him pass.
And onward through the open gate he came,
A leper with the ashes on his brow,
Sackcloth about his loins, and on his lip
A covering, stepping painfully and slow,
And with a difficult utterance, like one
Whose heart is like an iron nerve put down,
Crying, " Unclean ! unclean ! "

              'Twas now the first
Of the Judean autumn, and the leaves,
Whose shadows lay so still upon his path,
Had put their beauty forth beneath the eye
Of Judah's loftiest noble.   He was young,
And eminently beautiful, and life
Mantled in eloquent fulness on his lip
And sparkled in his glance, and in his mien
There was a gracious pride that every eye
Follow'd with benisons—and this was he !
With the soft airs of summer there had come
A torpor on his frame, which not the speed
Of his best barb, nor music, nor the blast
Of the bold huntsman's horn, nor aught that stirs
The spirit to its bent, might drive away.
The blood beat not as wont within his veins ;
Dimness crept o'er his eye ; a drowsy sloth
Fetter'd his limbs like palsy, and his mien,

With all its loftiness, seem'd struck with eld.
Even his voice was changed—a languid moan
Taking the place of the clear silver key ;
And brain and sense grew faint, as if the light
And very air were steep'd in sluggishness.
He strove with it awhile, as manhood will,
Ever too proud for weakness, till the rein
Slacken'd within his grasp, and in its poise
The arrowy jereed like an aspen shook.
Day after day, he lay as if in sleep.
His skin grew dry and bloodless, and white scales,
Circled with livid purple, cover'd him.
And then his nails grew black, and fell away
From the dull flesh about them, and the hues
Deepen'd beneath the hard unmoisten'd scales,
And from their edges grew the rank white hair,
—And Helon was a leper !

                Day was breaking
When at the altar of the Temple stood
The holy priest of God.   The incense lamp
Burn'd with a struggling light, and a low chant
Swell'd through the hollow arches of the roof
Like an articulate wail, and there, alone,
Wasted to ghastly thinness, Helon knelt.
The echoes of the melancholy strain
Died in the distant aisles, and he rose up,
Struggling with weakness, and bow'd down his head
Unto the sprinkled ashes, and put off
His costly raiment for the leper's garb ;
And with the sackcloth round him, and his lip
Hid in a loathsome covering, stood still,
Waiting to hear his doom :—

      Depart ! depart, O child
Of Israel, from the temple of thy God !

For He has smote thee with His chastening rod;
    And to the desert wild,
From all thou lov'st, away thy feet must flee,
That from thy plague His people may be free.

    Depart! and come not near
The busy mart, the crowded city, more;
Nor set thy foot a human threshold o'er;
    And stay thou not to hear
Voices that call thee in the way; and fly
From all who in the wilderness pass by.

    Wet not thy burning lip
In streams that to a human dwelling glide;
Nor rest thee where the covert fountains hide;
    Nor kneel thee down to dip
The water where the pilgrim bends to drink,
By desert well or river's grassy brink;

    And pass thou not between
The weary traveller and the cooling breeze;
And lie not down to sleep beneath the trees
    Where human tracks are seen;
Nor milk the goat that browseth on the plain,
Nor pluck the standing corn or yellow grain.

    And now depart! and when
Thy heart is heavy and thine eyes are dim,
Lift up thy prayer beseechingly to Him
    Who, from the tribes of men,
Selected thee to feel His chastening rod.
Depart! O leper! and forget not God!

And he went forth—alone! not one of all
The many whom he loved, nor she whose name
Was woven in the fibres of the heart
Breaking within him now, to come and speak

Comfort unto him.   Yea—he went his way,
Sick, and heart-broken, and alone—to die!
For God had cursed the leper!

It was noon,
And Helon knelt beside a stagnant pool
In the lone wilderness, and bathed his brow,
Hot with the burning leprosy, and touch'd
The loathsome water to his fever'd lips,
Praying that he might be so blest—to die!
Footsteps approach'd, and, with no strength to flee,
He drew the covering closer on his lip,
Crying, "Unclean! unclean!" and in the folds
Of the coarse sackcloth shrouding up his face,
He fell upon the earth till they should pass.
Nearer the Stranger came, and bending o'er
The leper's prostrate form, pronounced his name—
"Helon!"   The voice was like the master-tone
Of a rich instrument—most strangely sweet;
And the dull pulses of disease awoke,
And for a moment beat beneath the hot
And leprous scales with a restoring thrill.
"Helon! arise!" and he forgot his curse,
And rose and stood before Him.

Love and awe
Mingled in the regard of Helon's eye
As he beheld the Stranger.   He was not
In costly raiment clad, nor on His brow
The symbol of a princely lineage wore;
No followers at His back, nor in His hand
Buckler, or sword, or spear,—yet in His mien
Command sat throned serene, and if He smiled,
A kingly condescension graced His lips,
The lion would have crouch'd to in his lair.

His garb was simple, and His sandals worn ;
His stature modell'd with a perfect grace ;
His countenance the impress of a God,
Touch'd with the opening innocence of a child ;
His eye was blue and calm, as is the sky
In the serenest noon ; His hair, unshorn,
Fell to His shoulders, and His curling beard
The fulness of perfected manhood bore.
He look'd on Helon earnestly awhile,
As if His heart were moved, and stooping down,
He took a little water in His hand
And laid it on his brow, and said, " Be clean ! "
And lo ! the scales fell from him, and his blood
Coursed with delicious coolness through his veins,
And his dry palms grew moist, and on his brow
The dewy softness of an infant's stole.
His leprosy was cleansed, and he fell down
Prostrate at Jesus' feet and worshipp'd Him.

LAZARUS AND MARY.

(St. John xi.)

JESUS was there but yesterday. The prints
Of His departing feet were at the door ;
His " Peace be with you ! " was yet audible
In the rapt porch of Mary's charmed ear ;
And, in the low rooms, 'twas as if the air,
Hush'd with His going forth, had been the breath
Of angels left on watch—so conscious still
The place seem'd of His presence ! Yet, within,

D

The family by Jesus loved were weeping,
For Lazarus lay dead.

                              And Mary sat
By the pale sleeper. He was young to die.
The countenance whereon the Saviour dwelt
With His benignant smile—the soft fair lines
Breathing of hope—were still all eloquent,
Like life well mock'd in marble. That the voice,
Gone from those pallid lips, was heard in heaven,
Toned with unearthly sweetness—that the light,
Quench'd in the closing of those stirless lids,
Was veiling before God its timid fire,
New-lit, and brightening like a star at eve—
That Lazarus, her brother, was in bliss,
Not with this cold clay sleeping—Mary knew.
Her heaviness of heart was not for him!
But close had been the tie by Death divided.
The intertwining locks of that bright hair
That wiped the feet of Jesus—the fair hands
Clasp'd in her breathless wonder while He taught—
Scarce to one pulse thrill'd more in unison,
Than with one soul this sister and her brother
Had lock'd their lives together. In this love,
Hallow'd from stain, the woman's heart of Mary
Was, with its rich affections, all bound up.
Of an unblemish'd beauty, as became
An office by archangels fill'd till now,
She walk'd with a celestial halo clad ;
And while, to the Apostle's eyes, it seem'd
She but fulfill'd her errand out of heaven—
Sharing her low roof with the Son of God—
She was a woman, fond and mortal still ;
And the deep fervour, lost to passion's fire,
Breathed through the sister's tenderness. In vain
Knew Mary, gazing on that face of clay,

That it was not her brother. He was there —
Swathed in that linen vesture for the grave—
The same loved one in all his comeliness—
And with him to the grave her heart must go.
What though he talk'd of her to angels ? nay,
Hover'd in spirit near her ?—'twas that arm,
Palsied in death, whose fond caress she knew !
It was that lip of marble with whose kiss,
Morning and eve, love hemm'd the sweet day in.
This was the form by the Judean maids
Praised for its palm-like stature, as he walk'd
With her by Kedron in the eventide—
The dead was Lazarus !

.   .   .   .

The burial was over, and the night
Fell upon Bethany—and morn—and noon ;
And comforters and mourners went their way—
But Death stay'd on !   They had been oft alone,
When Lazarus had follow'd Christ to hear
His teachings in Jerusalem ; but this
Was more than solitude.   The silence now
Was void of expectation.   Something felt
Always before, and loved without a name,—
Joy from the air, hope from the opening door,
Welcome and life from off the very walls,—
Seem'd gone—and in the chamber where he lay
There was a fearful and unbreathing hush,
Stiller than night's last hour.   So fell on Mary
The shadows all have known, who, from their hearts,
Have released friends to heaven.   The parting soul
Spreads wing betwixt the mourner and the sky !
As if its path lay, from the tie last broken,
Straight through the cheering gateway of the sun ;
And, to the eye strain'd after, ' tis a cloud
That bars the light from all things.

                              Now as Christ
Drew near to Bethany, the Jews went forth
With Martha, mourning Lazarus. But Mary
Sat in the house. She knew the hour was nigh
When He would go again, as He had said,
Unto His Father; and she felt that He,
Who loved her brother Lazarus in life,
Had chose the hour to bring him home thro' Death
In no unkind forgetfulness.   Alone
She could lift up the bitter prayer to heaven,
"Thy will be done, O God!"—but that dear brother
Had fill'd the cup and broke the bread for Christ;
And ever, at the morn, when she had knelt
And wash'd those holy feet, came Lazarus
To bind His sandals on, and follow forth
With dropp'd eyes, like an angel, sad and fair—
Intent upon the Master's need alone.
Indissolubly link'd were they!   And now,
To go to meet Him—Lazarus not there—
And to His greeting answer "It is well!"
And, without tears, (since grief would trouble Him
Whose soul was always sorrowful,) to kneel
And minister alone—her heart gave way!
She cover'd up her face and turn'd again
To wait within for Jesus. But once more
Came Martha, saying, "Lo! the Lord is here
And calleth for thee, Mary!" Then arose
The mourner from the ground, whereon she sate
Shrouded in sackcloth, and bound quickly up
The golden locks of her dishevell'd hair,
And o'er her ashy garments drew a veil
Hiding the eyes she could not trust.   And still
As she made ready to go forth, a calm
As in a dream fell on her.

                              At a fount

Hard by the sepulchre, without the wall,
Jesus awaited Mary. Seated near
Were the way-worn disciples in the shade;
But, of Himself forgetful, Jesus lean'd
Upon His staff, and watch'd where she should come
To whose one sorrow—but a sparrow's falling—
The pity that redeem'd a world could bleed!
And, as she came, with that uncertain step,—
Eager, yet weak,—her hands upon her breast,—
And they who follow'd her all fallen back
To leave her with her sacred grief alone,—
The heart of Christ was troubled. She drew near,
And the disciples rose up from the fount,
Moved by her look of woe, and gather'd round;
And Mary—for a moment—ere she look'd
Upon the Saviour, stay'd her faltering feet,—
And straighten'd her veil'd form, and tighter drew
Her clasp upon the folds across her breast;
Then, with a vain strife to control her tears,
She stagger'd to their midst, and at His feet
Fell prostrate, saying, "Lord! hadst Thou been here,
My brother had not died!" The Saviour groan'd
In spirit, and stoop'd tenderly, and raised
The mourner from the ground, and in a voice,
Broke in its utterance like her own, He said,
"Where have ye laid him?" Then the Jews who came,
Following Mary, answer'd through their tears,
"Lord! come and see!" But lo! the mighty heart
That in Gethsemane sweat drops of blood,
Taking for us the cup that might not pass—
The heart whose breaking cord upon the cross
Made the earth tremble and the sun afraid
To look upon His agony—the heart
Of a lost world's Redeemer overflow'd,
Touch'd by a mourner's sorrow! Jesus wept.

Calm'd by those pitying tears, and fondly brooding
Upon the thought that Christ so loved her brother,
Stood Mary there; but that lost burden now
Lay on His heart who pitied her; and Christ,
Following slow, and groaning in Himself,
Came to the sepulchre. It was a cave,
And a stone lay upon it. Jesus said,
"Take ye away the stone!" Then lifted He
His moisten'd eyes to heaven, and while the Jews
And the disciples bent their heads in awe,
And trembling Mary sank upon her knees,
The Son of God pray'd audibly. He ceased,
And for a minute's space there was a hush,
As if th' angelic watchers of the world
Had stay'd the pulses of all breathing things
To listen to that prayer. The face of Christ
Shone as He stood, and over Him there came
Command, as 'twere the living face of God,
And with a loud voice He cried, "Lazarus!
Come forth!" And instantly, bound hand and foot,
And borne by unseen angels from the cave,
He that was dead stood with them. At the word
Of Jesus, the fear-stricken Jews unloosed
The bands from off the foldings of his shroud;
And Mary, with her dark veil thrown aside,
Ran to him swiftly, and cried, "LAZARUS!
MY BROTHER, LAZARUS!" and tore away
The napkin she had bound about his head—
And touch'd the warm lips with her fearful hand--
And on his neck fell weeping. And while all
Lay on their faces prostrate, Lazarus
Took Mary by the hand, and they knelt down
And worshipp'd Him who loved them.

SCENES IN GETHSEMANE.
(St. Matthew xxvi.)

THE moon was shining yet.   The Orient's brow,
Set with the morning-star, was not yet dim ;
And the deep silence which subdues the breath
Like a strong feeling, hung upon the world
As sleep upon the pulses of a child.
'Twas the last watch of night.   Gethsemane,
With its bathed leaves of silver, seem'd dissolved
In visible stillness ; and as Jesus' voice,
With its bewildering sweetness, met the ear
Of His disciples, it vibrated on
Like the first whisper in a silent world.
They came on slowly.   Heaviness oppress'd
The Saviour's heart, and when the kindnesses
Of His deep love were pour'd, He felt the need
Of near communion, for His gift of strength
Was wasted by the spirit's weariness.
He left them there and went a little on,
And in the depth of that hush'd silentness,
Alone with God, He fell upon His face ;
And as His heart was broken with the rush
Of His surpassing agony, and death,
Wrung to Him from a dying universe,
Was mightier than the Son of Man could bear,
He gave His sorrows way—and in the deep
Prostration of His soul, breathed out the prayer,
" Father, if it be possible with Thee,
Let this cup pass from Me."   Oh, how a word,
Like the forced drop before the fountain breaks,

Stilleth the press of human agony !
The Saviour felt its quiet in His soul ;
And though His strength was weakness, and the light
Which led Him on till now was sorely dim,
He breathed a new submission—"Not my will,
But Thine be done, O Father !"　As He spoke,
Voices were heard in heaven, and music stole
Out from the chambers of the vaulted sky,
As if the stars were swept like instruments.
No clouds were visible, but radiant wings
Were coming with a silvery rush to earth ;
And as the Saviour rose, a glorious one,
With an illumined forehead, and the light
Whose fountain is the mystery of God,
Encalm'd within his eye, bow'd down to Him,
And nerved Him with a ministry of strength.
It was enough—and with His Godlike brow
Re-written of His Father's messenger,
With meekness, whose divinity is more
Than power and glory, He return'd again
To His disciples, and awaked their sleep,
For " he that should betray Him was at hand."

RELIGIOUS POEMS.

RELIGIOUS POEMS.

—+—

TO MY MOTHER FROM THE APENNINES.

Mother ! dear mother ! the feelings nurst
As I hung at thy bosom, *clung round thee first.*
'Twas the earliest link in love's warm chain—
'Tis the only one that will long remain :
And as year by year, and day by day,
Some friend still trusted drops away,
Mother ! dear mother ! *oh, dost thou see*
How the shorten'd chain brings me nearer thee !
—EARLY POEMS.

'TIS midnight the lone mountains on—
  The East is fleck'd with cloudy bars,
And, gliding through them one by one,
  The moon walks up her path of stars—
The light upon her placid brow
Received from fountains unseen now.

And happiness is mine to-night,
  Thus springing from an unseen fount ;
And breast and brain are warm with light,
  With midnight round me on the mount —
Its rays, like thine, fair Dian, flow
From far that Western star below.

Dear mother ! in thy love I live ;
  The life thou gav'st flows yet from thee—
And, sun-like, thou hast power to give
  Life to the earth, air, sea, for me !
Though wandering, as this moon above,
I'm dark without thy constant love.

THE MOTHER TO HER CHILD.

THEY tell me thou art come from a far world,
Babe of my bosom ! that these little arms,
Whose restlessness is like the spread of wings,
Move with the memory of flights scarce o'er—
That through these fringed lids we see the soul
Steep'd in the blue of its remember'd home ;
And while thou sleep'st come messengers, they say,
Whispering to thee—and 'tis then I see
Upon thy baby lips that smile of heaven !

  And what is thy far errand, my fair child ?
Why away, wandering from a home of bliss,
To find thy way through darkness home again ?
Wert thou an untried dweller in the sky ?
Is there, betwixt the cherub that thou wert,
The cherub and the angel thou may'st be,
A life's probation in this sadder world ?
Art thou, with memory of two things only,
Music and light, left upon earth astray,
And by the watchers at the gate of heaven
Look'd for with fear and trembling ?

                              God ! who gavest
Into my guiding hand this wanderer,
To lead her through a world whose darkling paths
I tread with steps so faltering—leave not me
To bring her to the gates of heaven, alone !
I feel my feebleness.   Let *these* stay on—
The angels who now visit her in dreams !
Bid them be near her pillow till in death
The closed eyes look upon Thy face once more !
And let the light and music, which the world

Borrows of heaven, and which her infant sense
Hails with sweet recognition, be to her
A voice to call her upward, and a lamp
To lead her steps unto Thee

THIRTY-FIVE.

" The years of a man's life are threescore and ten."

Oh, weary heart ! thou'rt half-way home !
 We stand on life's meridian height—
As far from childhood's morning come,
 As to the grave's forgetful night.
Give Youth and Hope a parting tear—
 Look onward with a placid brow—
Hope promised but to bring us here,
 And Reason takes the guidance now—
One backward look—the last—the last !
One silent tear—for *Youth is past !*

Who goes with Hope and Passion back ?
 Who comes with me and Memory on ?
Oh, lonely looks the downward track—
 Joy's music hush'd—Hope's roses gone !
To Pleasure and her giddy troop
 Farewell, without a sigh or tear !
But heart gives way, and spirits droop,
 To think that Love may leave us here !
Have we no charm when Youth is flown—
Midway to death left sad and lone !

Yet stay !—as 'twere a twilight star
 That sends its threads across the wave,
I see a brightening light, from far,
 Steal down a path beyond the grave !

And now—bless God !—its golden line
  Comes o'er, and lights my shadowy way,
And shows the dear hand clasp'd in mine.
  But list what those sweet voices say :
      The better land's in sight,
      And, by its chastening light,
    All love from life's midway is driven,
Save hers whose clasped hand will bring thee on to heaven.

THE SABBATH.

It was a pleasant morning, in the time
When the leaves fall, and the bright sun shone out
As when the morning stars first sang together—
So quietly and calmly fell his light
Upon a world at rest.   There was no leaf
In motion, and the loud winds slept, and all
Was still.   The lab'ring herd was grazing
Upon the hill-side quietly—uncall'd
By the harsh voice of man ; and distant sound,
Save from the murmuring waterfall, came not
As usual on the ear.   One hour stole on,
And then another of the morning, calm
And still as Eden ere the birth of man.
And then broke in the Sabbath chime of bells—
And the old man and his descendants went
Together to the house of God.   I join'd
The well-apparell'd crowd.   The holy man
Rose solemnly, and breathed the prayer of faith—
And the grey saint, just on the wing for heaven—
And the fair maid—and the bright-hair'd young man—
And child of curling locks, just taught to close
The lash of its blue eye the while ;—all knelt

In attitude of prayer—and then the hymn,
Sincere in its low melody, went up
To worship God.

        The white-hair'd pastor rose
And look'd upon his flock, and with an eye
That told his interest, and voice that spoke
In tremulous accents eloquence like Paul's,
He lent Isaiah's fire to the truths
Of revelation, and persuasion came
Like gushing waters from his lips, till hearts
Unused to bend were soften'd, and the eye
Unwont to weep sent forth the willing tear.

I went my way—but as I went, I thought
How holy was the Sabbath-day of God.

ON THE DEATH OF A MISSIONARY.

How beautiful it is for man to die
Upon the walls of Zion ! to be call'd,
Like a watch-worn and weary sentinel,
To put his armour off, and rest—in heaven !

The sun was setting on Jerusalem,
The deep blue sky had not a cloud, and light
Was pouring on the dome of Omar's mosque
Like molten silver.   Everything was fair ;
And beauty hung upon the painted fanes,
Like a grieved spirit, lingering ere she gave
Her wing to air, for heaven.   The crowds of men
Were in the busy streets, and nothing look'd
Like woe or suffering, save one small train
Bearing the dead to burial.   It pass'd by,

And left no trace upon the busy throng.
The sun was just as beautiful; the shout
Of joyous revelry, and the low hum
Of stirring thousands rose as constantly!
Life look'd as winning; and the earth and sky,
And everything seem'd strangely bent to make
A contrast to that comment upon life.
How wonderful it is that human pride
Can pass that touching moral as it does—
Pass it so frequently, in all the force
Of mournful and most simple eloquence—
And learn no lesson! They bore on the dead,
With the slow step of sorrow, troubled not
By the rude multitude, save, here and there,
A look of vague inquiry, or a curse
Half-mutter'd by some haughty Turk whose sleeve
Had touch'd the tassel of the Christian's pall.
And Israel too pass'd on—the trampled Jew!
Israel!—who made Jerusalem a throne
For the wide world—pass'd on as carelessly,
Giving no look of interest to tell
The shrouded dead was anything to her.
Oh, that they would be gather'd as a brood
Is gather'd by a parent's sheltering wings!

They laid him down with strangers, for his home
Was with the setting sun, and they who stood
And look'd so steadfastly upon his grave
Were not his kindred; but they found him there,
And loved him for his ministry of Christ.
He had died young; but there are silver'd heads
Whose race of duty is less nobly run.
His heart was with Jerusalem; and strong
As was a mother's love, and the sweet ties
Religion makes so beautiful at home,

He flung them from him in his eager race,
And sought the broken people of his God,
To preach to them of JESUS.   There was one
Who was his friend and helper—one who went
And knelt beside him at the sepulchre
Where Jesus slept, to pray for Israel.
They had one spirit, and their hearts were knit
With more than human love.   God call'd him home,
And he of whom I speak stood up alone,
And in his broken-heartedness wrought on
Until his Master call'd him.

Oh, is it not a noble thing to die,
As dies the Christian, with his armour on ?
What is the hero's clarion, though its blast
Ring with the mastery of a world, to this ?—
What are the searching victories of mind—
The lore of vanish'd ages ?—What are all
The trumpetings of proud humanity,
To the short history of him who made
His sepulchre beside the King of kings ?

ON WITNESSING A BAPTISM.

SHE stood up in the meekness of a heart
Resting on God, and held her fair young child
Upon her bosom, with its gentle eyes
Folded in sleep, as if its soul had gone
To whisper the baptismal vow in heaven.
The prayer went up devoutly, and the lips
Of the good man glow'd fervently with faith
That it would be, even as he had pray'd,
And the sweet child be gather'd to the fold
Of Jesus.   As the holy words went on,

E

Her lips moved silently, and tears, fast tears,
Stole from beneath her lashes, and upon
The forehead of the beautiful child lay soft
With the baptismal water.   Then I thought
That, to the eye of God, that mother's tears
Would be a deeper covenant—which sin,
And the temptations of the world, and death,
Would leave unbroken—and that she would know,
In the clear light of heaven, how very strong
The prayer which press'd them from her heart had been,
In leading its young spirit up to God.

CONTEMPLATION.

"THEY are all up—the innumerable stars—
And hold their place in heaven.   My eyes have been
Searching the pearly depths through which they spring
Like beautiful creations, till I feel
As if it were a new and perfect world,
Waiting in silence for the word of God
To breathe it into motion.   There they stand,
Shining in order, like a living hymn
Written in light, awakening at the breath
Of the celestial dawn, and praising Him
Who made them, with the harmony of spheres.
I would I had an eagle's ear to list
That melody.   I would that I might float
Up in that boundless element, and feel
Its ravishing vibrations, like the pulse
Beating in heaven !   My spirit is athirst
For music—rarer music !   I would bathe
My soul in a serener atmosphere
Than this ; I long to mingle with the flock

Led by the 'living waters,' and to stray
In the 'green pastures' of the better land!
When wilt thou break, dull fetter? When shall I
Gather my wings, and like a rushing thought
Stretch onward, star by star, up into heaven?"
Thus mused Alethe. She was one to whom
Life had been like the witching of a dream,
Of an untroubled sweetness. She was born
Of a high race, and lay upon the knee,
With her soft eyes perusing listlessly
The fretted roof, or, on mosaic floors,
Grasped at the tesselated squares inwrought
With metals curiously. Her childhood pass'd
Like a fairy—amid fountains and green haunts—
Trying her little feet upon a lawn
Of velvet evenness, and hiding flowers
In her sweet breast, as if it were a fair
And pearly altar to crush incense on.
Her youth—oh! that was queenly! She was like
A dream of poetry that may not be
Written or told—exceeding beautiful!
And so came worshippers; and rank bow'd down
And breathed upon her heart-strings with the breath
Of pride, and bound her forehead gorgeously
With dazzling scorn, and gave unto her step
A majesty as if she trod the sea,
And the proud waves, unbidden, lifted her!
And so she grew to woman—her mere look
Strong as a monarch's signet, and her hand
The ambition of a kingdom. From all this
Turn'd her high heart away! She had a mind,
Deep and immortal, and it would not feed
On pageantry. She thirsted for a spring
Of a serener element, and drank
Philosophy, and for a little while

She was allay'd—till, presently, it turn'd
Bitter within her, and her spirit grew
Faint for undying water.   Then she came
To the pure fount of God, and is athirst
No more—save when the fever of the world
Falleth upon her, she will go, sometimes,
Out in the starlight quietness, and breathe
A holy aspiration after heaven.

THE BELFRY PIGEON.

ON the cross-beam under the Old South bell
The nest of a pigeon is builded well.
In summer and winter that bird is there,
Out and in with the morning air;
I love to see him track the street,
With his wary eye and active feet;
And I often watch him as he springs,
Circling the steeple with easy wings,
Till across the dial his shade has pass'd,
And the belfry edge is gain'd at last.
'Tis a bird I love, with its brooding note,
And the trembling throb in its mottled throat;
There's a human look in its swelling breast,
And the gentle curve of its lowly crest;
And I often stop with the fear I feel—
He runs so close to the rapid wheel.

Whatever is rung on that noisy bell—
Chime of the hour or funeral knell—
The dove in the belfry must hear it well.
When the tongue swings out to the midnight moon—
When the sexton cheerily rings for noon—

When the clock strikes clear at morning light—
When the child is waked with " nine at night"—
When the chimes play soft in the Sabbath air,
Filling the spirit with tones of prayer—
Whatever tale in the bell is heard,
He broods on his folded feet unstirr'd,
Or, rising half in his rounded nest,
He takes the time to smooth his breast,
Then drops again with filmed eyes,
And sleeps as the last vibration dies.
Sweet bird ! I would that I could be
A hermit in the crowd like thee !
With wings to fly to wood and glen.
Thy lot, like mine, is cast with men ;
And daily, with unwilling feet,
I tread, like thee, the crowded street ;
But, unlike me, when day is o'er,
Thou canst dismiss the world and soar,
Or, at a half-felt wish for rest,
Canst smooth the feathers on thy breast,
And drop, forgetful, to thy nest.

DEDICATION HYMN.

[Written to be sung at the consecration of the Hanover Street
Church, Boston.]

THE perfect world by Adam trod
Was the first temple—built by God ;
His fiat laid the corner-stone,
And heaved its pillars, one by one.

He hung its starry roof on high—
The broad illimitable sky ;

He spread its pavement, green and bright,
And curtain'd it with morning light.

The mountains in their places stood—
The sea—the sky—and " all was good ; "
And, when its first pure praises rang,
The " morning stars together sang."

Lord ! 'tis not ours to make the sea
And earth and sky a house for Thee ;
But in Thy sight our off'ring stands—
A humbler temple, " made with hands."

———

THOUGHTS WHILE MAKING THE GRAVE OF A NEW-BORN CHILD.

Room, gentle flowers ! my child would pass to heaven !
Ye look'd not for her yet with your soft eyes,
O watchful ushers at Death's narrow door !
But lo ! while you delay to let her forth,
Angels, beyond, stay for her !   One long kiss
From lips all pale with agony, and tears,
Wrung after anguish had dried up with fire
The eyes that wept them, were the cup of life
Held as a welcome to her.   Weep ! O mother !
But not that from this cup of bitterness
A cherub of the sky has turn'd away.

One look upon thy face ere thou depart !
My daughter !   It is soon to let thee go !
My daughter !   With thy birth has gush'd a spring
I knew not of—filling my heart with tears,
And turning with strange tenderness to thee—

A love—O God ! it seems so—that must flow
Far as thou fleest, and 'twixt heaven and me,
Henceforward, be a bright and yearning chain
Drawing me after thee !   And so, farewell !
'Tis a harsh world, in which affection knows
No place to treasure up its loved and lost
But the foul grave !   Thou, who so late wast sleeping
Warm in the close fold of a mother's heart,
Scarce from her breast a single pulse receiving
But it was sent thee with some tender thought,
How can I leave thee—*here !*   Alas for man !
The herb in its humility may fall
And waste into the bright and genial air,
While we, by hands that minister'd in life
Nothing but love to us, are thrust away—
The earth flung in upon our just cold bosoms,
And the warm sunshine trodden out for ever !

Yet have I chosen for thy grave, my child,
A bank where I have lain in summer hours,
And thought how little it would seem like death
To sleep amid such loveliness.   The brook,
Tripping with laughter down the rocky steps
That lead up to thy bed, would still trip on,
Breaking the dread hush of the mourners gone ;
The birds are never silent that build here,
Trying to sing down the more vocal waters :
The slope is beautiful with moss and flowers,
And far below, seen under arching leaves,
Glitters the warm sun on the village spire,
Pointing the living after thee.   And this
Seems like a comfort ; and, replacing now
The flowers that have made room for thee, I go
To whisper the same peace to her who lies—
Robb'd of her child and lonely.   'Tis the work

Of many a dark hour, and of many a prayer,
To bring the heart back from an infant gone.
Hope must give o'er, and busy fancy blot
The images from all the silent rooms,
And every sight and sound familiar to her
Undo its sweetest link—and so at last
The fountain—that, once struck, must flow for ever—
Will hide and waste in silence.   When the smile
Steals to her pallid lip again, and spring
Wakens the buds above thee, we will come,
And, standing by thy music-haunted grave,
Look on each other cheerfully, and say :—
A child that we have loved is gone to heaven,
And by this gate of flowers she pass'd away !

A THOUGHT OVER A CRADLE.

I SADDEN when thou smilest to my smile,
Child of my love !   I tremble to believe
That o'er the mirror of that eye of blue
The shadow of my heart will always pass ;—
A heart that, from its struggle with the world,
Comes nightly to thy guarded cradle home,
And, careless of the staining dust it brings,
Asks for its idol !   Strange, that flowers of earth
Are visited by every air that stirs,
And drink its sweetness only, while the child
That shuts within its breast a bloom for heaven,
May take a blemish from the breath of love,
And bear the blight for ever.

                 I have wept
With gladness at the gift of this fair child !
My life is bound up in her.   But, O God !

Thou know'st how heavily my heart at times
Bears its sweet burthen; and if Thou hast given
To nurture such as mine this spotless flower,
To bring it unpolluted unto Thee,
Take Thou its love, I pray thee! Give it light—
Though, following the sun, it turn from me!—
But, by the chord thus wrung, and by the light
Shining about her, draw me to my child!
And link us close, O God, when near to heaven!

ON THE PICTURE OF A "CHILD TIRED OF PLAY."

TIRED of play! Tired of play!
What hast thou done this livelong day!
The birds are silent, and so is the bee;
The sun is creeping up steeple and tree;
The doves have flown to the sheltering eaves,
And the nests are dark with the drooping leaves;
Twilight gathers, and day is done—
How hast thou spent it—restless one?

Playing? But what hast thou done beside
To tell thy mother at eventide?
What promise of morn is left unbroken?
What kind word to thy playmate spoken?
Whom hast thou pitied, and whom forgiven?
How with thy faults has duty striven?
What hast thou learn'd by field and hill,
By greenwood path, and by singing rill?

There will come an eve to a longer day,
That will find thee tired—but not of play!

And thou wilt lean, as thou leanest now,
With drooping limbs and aching brow,
And wish the shadows would faster creep,
And long to go to thy quiet sleep.
Well were it then if thine aching brow
Were as free from sin and shame as now !
Well for thee if thy lip could tell
A tale like this, of a day spent well.
If thine open hand hath relieved distress—
If thy pity hath sprung to wretchedness—
If thou hast forgiven the sore offence,
And humbled thy heart with penitence—
If Nature's voices have spoken to thee
With her holy meanings eloquently—
If every creature hath won thy love,
From the creeping worm to the brooding dove—
If never a sad, low-spoken word
Hath pled with thy human heart unheard—
Then, when the night steals on, as now,
It will bring relief to thine aching brow,
And, with joy and peace at the thought of rest,
Thou wilt sink to sleep on thy mother's breast.

TO A CITY PIGEON.

Stoop to my window, thou beautiful dove !
Thy daily visits have touch'd my love ;
I watch thy coming, and list the note
That stirs so low in thy mellow throat,
    And my joy is high
To catch the glance of thy gentle eye.

Why dost thou sit on the heated eaves,
And forsake the wood with its freshen'd leaves?
Why dost thou haunt the sultry street,
When the paths of the forest are cool and sweet?
  How canst thou bear
This noise of people—this sultry air?

Thou alone of the feather'd race
Dost looked unscared on the human face;
Thou alone, with a wing to flee,
Dost love with man in his haunts to be;
  And the " gentle dove "
Has become a name for trust and love.

A holy gift is thine, sweet bird!
Thou'rt named with childhood's earliest word!
Thou'rt link'd with all that is fresh and wild
In the prison'd thoughts of the city child;
  And thy glossy wings
Are its brightest image of moving things.

It is no light chance. Thou art set apart,
Wisely by Him who has tamed thy heart,
To stir the love for the bright and fair
That else were seal'd in this crowded air;
  I sometimes dream
Angelic rays from thy pinions stream.

Come then, ever, when daylight leaves
The page I read, to my humble eaves,
And wash thy breast in the hollow spout,
And murmur thy low sweet music out!
  I hear and see
Lessons of heaven, sweet bird, in thee!

A CHILD'S FIRST IMPRESSION OF A STAR.

SHE had been told that God made all the stars
That twinkled up in heaven, and now she stood
Watching the coming of the twilight on,
As if it were a new and perfect world,
And this were its first eve.   She stood alone
By the low window, with the silken lash
Of her soft eye upraised, and her sweet mouth
Half parted with the new and strange delight
Of beauty that she could not comprehend,
And had not seen before.   The purple folds
Of the low sunset clouds, and the blue sky
That look'd so still and delicate above,
Fill'd her young heart with gladness, and the eve
Stole on with its deep shadows, and she still
Stood looking at the west with that half smile,
As if a pleasant thought were at her heart.
Presently, in the edge of the last tint
Of sunset, where the blue was melted in
To the faint golden mellowness, a star
Stood suddenly.   A laugh of wild delight
Burst from her lips, and putting up her hands,
Her simple thought broke forth expressively—
" Father ! dear father ! God has made a star ! "

LINES ON LEAVING EUROPE.

BRIGHT flag at yonder tapering mast !
  Fling out your field of azure blue ;
Let star and stripe be westward cast,
  And point as Freedom's eagle flew !
Strain home ! O lithe and quivering spars !
Point home, my country's flag of stars !

The wind blows fair ! the vessel feels
  The pressure of the rising breeze,
And, swiftest of a thousand keels,
  She leaps to the careering seas !
Oh, fair, fair cloud of snowy sail,
  In whose white breast I seem to lie,
How oft, when blew this eastern gale,
  I've seen your semblance in the sky,
And long'd with breaking heart to flee
On cloud-like pinions o'er the sea !

Adieu ! O lands of fame and eld !
  I turn to watch our foamy track,
And thoughts with which I first beheld
  Yon clouded line come hurrying back ;
My lips are dry with vague desire,
  My cheek once more is hot with joy—
My pulse, my brain, my soul on fire !—
  Oh, what has changed that traveller-boy ?
As leaves the ship this dying foam,
His visions fade behind—his weary heart speeds home

Adieu ! O soft and southern shore,
  Where dwelt the stars long miss'd in heaven—

Those forms of beauty seen no more,
 Yet once to Art's rapt vision given !
Oh, still th' enamour'd sun delays,
 And pries through fount and crumbling fane,
To win to his adoring gaze
 Those children of the sky again !
Irradiate beauty, such as never
 That light on other earth hath shone,
Hath made this land her home for ever;
 And could I live for this alone—
Were not my birthright brighter far
 Than such voluptuous slaves' can be—
Held not the West one glorious star,
 New-born and blazing for the free—
Soar'd not to heaven our eagle yet—
Rome, with her Helot sons, should teach me to forget !

Adieu ! O fatherland ! I see
 Your white cliffs on th' horizon's rim,
And though to freer skies I flee,
 My heart swells, and my eyes are dim !
As knows the dove the task you give her,
 When loosed upon a foreign shore—
As spreads the raindrop in the river
 In which it may have flow'd before—
To England, over vale and mountain,
 My fancy flew from climes more fair—
My blood, that knew its parent fountain,
 Ran warm and fast in England's air.

Dear mother ! in thy prayer to-night
 There come new words and warmer tears !
On long, long darkness breaks the light—
 Comes home the loved, the lost for years !

Sleep safe, O wave-worn mariner !
   Fear not to-night or storm or sea !
The ear of Heaven bends low to *her !*
   He comes to shore who sails with me !
The spider knows the roof unriven,
   While swings his web, though lightnings blaze—
And by a thread still fast on Heaven,
   I know my mother lives and prays !

Dear mother ! when our lips can speak—
   When first our tears will let us see—
When I can gaze upon thy cheek,
   And thou, with thy dear eyes, on me—
'Twill be a pastime little sad
   To trace what weight Time's heavy fingers
Upon each other's forms have had—
   For all may flee, so feeling lingers !
But there's a change, beloved mother !
   To stir far deeper thoughts of thine ;
I come, but with me comes another
   To share the heart once only mine !
Thou, on whose thoughts, when sad and lonely,
   One star arose in memory's heaven—
Thou, who hast watch'd *one* treasure only—
   Water'd *one* flower with tears at even—
Room in thy heart ! The hearth she left
   Is darken'd to lend light to ours !
There are bright flowers of care bereft,
   And hearts that languish more than flowers !
She was their light—their very air—
Room, mother, in thy heart ! place for her in thy prayer !

ON THE DEPARTURE OF REV. MR. WHITE
FROM HIS PARISH,

WHEN CHOSEN PRESIDENT OF WABASH COLLEGE.

LEAVE us not, man of prayer !   Like Paul, hast thou
" Served God with all humility of mind,"
Dwelling among us, and " with many tears,"
" From house to house," " by night and day not ceasing,"
Hast pleaded thy blest errand.   Leave us not !
Leave us not now !   The Sabbath-bell, so long
Link'd with thy voice—the prelude to thy prayer—
The call to us from heaven to come with thee
Into the house of God, and, from thy lips,
Hear what had fall'n upon thy heart—will sound
Lonely and mournfully when thou art gone !
Our prayers are in thy words—our hope in Christ
Warm'd on thy lips—our darkling thoughts of God
Follow'd thy loved call upward—and so knit
Is all our worship with those outspread hands,
And the imploring voice, which, well we knew,
Sank in the ear of Jesus—that, with thee,
The angel's ladder seems removed from sight,
And we astray in darkness !   Leave us not !
Leave not the dead !   They have lain calmly down—
Thy comfort in their ears—believing well
That when thine own more holy work was done,
Thou wouldst lie down beside them, and be near
When the last trump shall summon, to fold up
Thy flock affrighted, and, with that same voice
Whose whisper'd promises could sweeten death,
Take up once more the interrupted strain,
And wait Christ's coming, saying, " Here am I,

And those whom Thou hast given me !"   Leave not
The old, who, 'mid the gathering shadows, cling
To their accustom'd staff, and know not how
To lose thee, and so near the darkest hour !
Leave not the penitent, whose soul may be
Deaf to the strange voice, but awake to thine !
Leave not the mourner thou hast sooth'd—the heart
Turns to its comforter again !   Leave not
The child thou hast baptized ! another's care
May not keep bright, upon the mother's heart,
The covenant seal ; the infant's ear has caught
Words it has strangely ponder'd from thy lips,
And the remember'd tone may find again,
And quicken for the harvest, the first seed
Sown for eternity !   Leave not the child !

Yet, if thou wilt—if, " bound in spirit," thou
Must go, and we shall see thy face no more,
" The will of God be done ! "   We do not say
Remember us : thou wilt—in love and prayer !
And thou wilt be remember'd—by *the dead*,
When the last trump awakes them—by *the old*,
When of the " silver cord," whose strength thou knowest,
The last thread fails—by *the bereaved and stricken*,
When the dark cloud, wherein thou found'st a spot
Broke by the light of mercy, lowers again—
By *the sad mother*, pleading for her child,
In murmurs difficult, since thou art gone—
By *all thou leavest*, when the Sabbath-bell
Brings us together, and the closing hymn
Hushes our hearts to pray, and thy loved voice,
That all our wants had grown to, (only thus,
'Twould seem, articulate to God,) falls not
Upon our listening ears.   Remember'd thus—
Remember'd well—in all our holiest hours—

F

Will be the faithful shepherd we have lost !
And ever with one prayer, for which our love
Will find the pleading words,—that in the light
Of heaven we may behold his face once more !

———

A TRUE INCIDENT.

UPON a summer's morn, a Southern mother
Sat at the curtain'd window of an inn.
She rested from long travel, and, with hand
Upon her cheek in tranquil happiness,
Look'd where the busy travellers went and came ;
And, like the shadows of the swallows flying
Over the bosom of unruffled water,
Pass'd from her thoughts all objects, leaving there,
As in the water's breast, a mirror'd heaven—
For, in the porch beneath her, to and fro,
A nurse walk'd singing with her babe in arms.
And many a passer-by look'd on the child
And praised its wondrous beauty ; but still on
The old nurse troll'd her lullaby, and still,
Blest through her depths of soul by light there shining,
The mother in her reverie mused on.
But lo ! another traveller alighted !
And now, no more indifferent or calm,
The mother's breath comes quick, and, with the blood
Warm in her cheek and brow, she murmurs low,
"Now, God be praised ! I am no more alone
In knowing I've an angel for my child,—
Chance he to look on't only ! "   With a smile—
The tribute of a beauty-loving heart
To things from God new-moulded—would have pass'd
The poet, as the infant caught his eye ;

But suddenly he turn'd, and, with his hand
Upon the nurse's arm, he stay'd her steps,
And gazed upon her burthen.   'Twas a child
In whose large eyes of blue there shone, indeed,
Something to waken wonder.   Never sky
In noontide depth or softly-breaking dawn—
Never the dew in new-born violet's cup,
Lay so entranced in purity !   Not calm,
With the mere hush of infancy at rest,
The ample forehead, but serene with thought ;
And by the rapt expression of the lips,
They seemed scarce still from a cherubic hymn :
And over all its countenance there breathed
Benignity, majestic as we dream
Angels wear ever before God.   With gaze
Earnest and mournful, and his eyelids warm
With tears kept back, the poet kiss'd the child ;
And chasten'd at his heart, as having pass'd
Close to an angel, went upon his way.

Soon after, to the broken choir in heaven
This cherub was recall'd, and now the mother
Bethought her, in her anguish, of the bard—
(Herself a far-off stranger, but his heart
Familiar to the world,)—and wrote to tell him,
The angel he had recognised that morn
Had fled to bliss again.   The poet well
Remember'd that child's ministry to him ;
And of the only fountain that he knew
For healing, he sought comfort for the mother.
And thus he wrote :—
Mourn not for the child from thy tenderness riven,
Ere stain on its purity fell !
To thy questioning heart, lo ! an answer from heaven :
" Is it well with the child ? "—" It is well ! "

BIRTHDAY VERSES.

"The heart that we have lain near before our birth, is the only one that
cannot forget that it has loved us."—Philip Slingsby.

My birthday!—O beloved mother!
    My heart is with thee o'er the seas.
I did not think to count another
    Before I wept upon thy knees—
Before this scroll of absent years
Was blotted with thy streaming tears.

My own I do not care to check.
    I weep—albeit here alone—
As if I hung upon thy neck,
    As if thy lips were on my own,
As if this full, sad heart of mine
Were beating closely upon thine.

Four weary years!   How looks she now?
    What light is in those tender eyes?
What trace of time has touch'd the brow
    Whose look is borrow'd of the skies
That listen to her nightly prayer?
How is she changed since *he* was there?

Who sleeps upon her heart alway—
    Whose name upon her lips is worn—
For whom the night seems made to pray—
    For whom she wakes to pray at morn—
Whose sight is dim, whose heart-strings stir
Who weeps these tears—to think of *her!*

I know not if my mother's eyes
  Would find me changed in slighter things;
I've wander'd beneath many skies,
  And tasted of some bitter springs;
And many leaves, once fair and gay,
From youth's full flower have dropp'd away—
But, as these looser leaves depart,
  The lessen'd flower gets near the core,
And, when deserted quite, the heart
  Takes closer what was dear of yore—
And yearns to those who loved it first—
The sunshine and the dew by which its bud was nursed.

Dear mother! dost thou love me yet?
  Am I remember'd in my home?
When those I love for joy are met,
  Does some one wish that I would come?
Thou *dost*—I *am* beloved of these!
  But, as the schoolboy numbers o'er
Night after night the Pleiades
  And finds the stars he found before—
As turns the maiden oft her token—
  As counts the miser aye his gold—
So, till life's silver cord is broken,
  Would I of thy fond love be told.
My heart is full, mine eyes are wet—
Dear mother! dost thou love thy long-lost wanderer
    yet?

Oh! when the hour to meet again
  Creeps on—and, speeding o'er the sea,
My heart takes up its lengthen'd chain,
  And link by link draws nearer thee—
When land is hail'd, and from the shore
  Comes off the blessed breath of home,

With fragrance from my mother's door
　Of flowers forgotten when I come—
When port is gain'd, and, slowly now,
　The old familiar paths are pass'd,
And, entering—unconscious how—
　I gaze upon thy face at last,
And run to thee, all faint and weak,
And feel thy tears upon my cheek—
　Oh ! if my heart break not with joy,
The light of heaven will fairer seem ;
　And I shall grow once more a boy :
And, mother !—'twill be like a dream
　That we were parted thus for years—
　And, once that we have dried our tears,
　How will the days seem long and bright—
To meet thee always with the morn,
　And hear thy blessing every night—
Thy " dearest," thy " first-born ! "—
And be no more, as now, in a strange land forlorn !

SATURDAY AFTERNOON.

[*Written for a Picture.*]

I LOVE to look on a scene like this,
　Of wild and careless play,
And persuade myself that I am not old,
　And my locks are not yet grey ;
For it stirs the blood in an old man's heart,
　And makes his pulses fly,
To catch the thrill of a happy voice,
　And the light of a pleasant eye.

I have walk'd the world for fourscore years ;
　And they say that I am old,
That my heart is ripe for the reaper, Death,
　And my years are well-nigh told.
It is very true—it is very true ;
　I'm old, and " I bide my time : "
But my heart will leap at a scene like this,
　And I half renew my prime.

Play on, play on ; I am with you there,
　In the midst of your merry ring ;
I can feel the thrill of the daring jump,
　And the rush of the breathless swing.
I hide with you in the fragrant hay,
　And I whoop the smother'd call,
And my feet slip up on the seedy floor,
　And I care not for the fall.

I am willing to die when my time shall come,
　And I shall be glad to go ;
For the world at best is a weary place,
　And my pulse is getting low ;
But the grave is dark, and the heart will fail
　In treading its gloomy way ;
And it wiles my heart from its dreariness
　To see the young so gay.

———

REVERIE AT GLENMARY.

I HAVE enough, O God ! My heart to-night
Runs over with its fulness of content ;
And as I look out on the fragrant stars,
And from the beauty of the night take in

My priceless portion—yet myself no more
Than in the universe a grain of sand—
I feel His glory who could make a world,
Yet in the lost depths of the wilderness
Leave not a flower unfinish'd !

      Rich, though poor !
My low-roof'd cottage is this hour a heaven.
Music is in it—and the song she sings,
That sweet-voiced wife of mine, arrests the ear
Of my young child awake upon her knee ;
And with his calm eye on his master's face,
My noble hound lies couchant—and all here—
All in this little home, yet boundless heaven—
Are, in such love as I have power to give,
Blessed to overflowing.

      Thou, who look'st
Upon my brimming heart this tranquil eve,
Knowest its fulness, as Thou dost the dew
Sent to the hidden violet by Thee ;
And, as that flower, from its unseen abode,
Sends its sweet breath up, duly, to the sky,
Changing its gift to incense, so, O God !
May the sweet drops that to my humble cup
Find their far way from heaven, send up, to Thee,
Fragrance at Thy throne welcome !

COLLEGE POEMS.

COLLEGE POEMS.

———✦———

EXTRACT

*From a Poem delivered at the Departure of the Senior Class of
Yale College in* 1827.

.   .   .   .

WE shall go forth together. There will come
Alike the day of trial unto all,
And the rude world will buffet us alike.
Temptation hath a music for all ears;
And mad ambition trumpeteth to all;
And the ungovernable thought within
Will be in every bosom eloquent;—
But when the silence and the calm come on,
And the high seal of character is set,
We shall not all be similar. The flow
Of lifetime is a graduated scale;
And deeper than the vanities of power,
Or the vain pomp of glory, there is writ
A standard measuring its worth for heaven.
The pathway to the grave may be the same,
And the proud man shall tread it, and the low,
With his bow'd head, shall bear him company.
Decay will make no difference, and Death,
With his cold hand, shall make no difference;
And there will be no precedence of power
In waking at the coming trump of God;

But in the temper of the invisible mind,
The godlike and undying intellect,
There are distinctions that will live in heaven,
When time is a forgotten circumstance !
The elevated brow of kings will lose
The impress of regalia, and the slave
Will wear his immortality as free,
Beside the crystal waters ; but the depth
Of glory in the attributes of God
Will measure the capacities of mind ;
And as the angels differ, will the ken
Of gifted spirits glorify him more.
It is life's mystery.   The soul of man
Createth its own destiny of power ;
And, as the trial is intenser here,
His being hath a nobler strength in heaven.

What is its earthly victory ?   Press on !
For it hath tempted angels.   Yet press on !
For it shall make you mighty among men ;
And from the eyrie of your eagle thought,
Ye shall look down on monarchs.   Oh, press on !
For the high ones and powerful shall come
To do you reverence, and the beautiful
Will know the purer language of your brow,
And read it like a talisman of love !
Press on ! for it is godlike to unloose
The spirit, and forget yourself in thought ;
Bending a pinion for the deeper sky,
And, in the very fetters of your flesh,
Mating with the pure essences of heaven !
Press on !—" for in the grave there is no work,
And no device."   Press on ! while yet ye may !

So lives the soul of man.   It is the thirst

Of his immortal nature ; and he rends
The rock for secret fountains, and pursues
The path of the illimitable wind
For mysteries—and this is human pride !
There is a gentler element, and man
May breathe it with a calm, unruffled soul,
And drink its living waters till his heart
Is pure—and this is human happiness !
Its secret and its evidence are writ
In the broad book of Nature.　'Tis to have
Attentive and believing faculties ;
To go abroad rejoicing in the joy
Of beautiful and well-created things ;
To love the voice of waters, and the sheen
Of silver fountains leaping to the sea ;
To thrill with the rich melody of birds,
Living their life of music ; to be glad
In the gay sunshine, reverent in the storm ;
To see a beauty in the stirring leaf,
And find calm thoughts beneath the whispering tree ;
To see, and hear, and breathe the evidence
Of God's deep wisdom in the natural world !
It is to linger on " the magic face
Of human beauty," and from light and shade
Alike to draw a lesson ; 'tis to love
The cadences of voices that are tuned
By majesty and purity of thought ;
To gaze on woman's beauty, as a star
Whose purity and distance make it fair ;
And in the gush of music to be still,
And feel that it has purified the heart !
It is to love all virtue for itself,
All nature for its breathing evidence ;
And, when the eye hath seen, and when the ear
Hath drunk the beautiful harmony of the world,

It is to humble the imperfect mind,
And lean the broken spirit upon God !

Thus would I, at this parting hour, be true
To the great moral of a passing world.
Thus would I—like a just-departing child,
Who lingers on the threshold of his home—
Remember the best lesson of the lips
Whose accents shall be with us now, no more !
And I would press the lesson ; that, when life
Hath half become a weariness, and hope
Thirsts for serener waters, go abroad
Upon the paths of Nature, and, when all
Its voices whisper, and its silent things
Are breathing the deep beauty of the world,
Kneel at its simple altar, and the God
Who hath the living waters shall be there !

EXTRACTS

From a Poem delivered at Brown University in 1830.

WHAT is *ambition ?* 'Tis a glorious cheat !
Angels of light walk not so dazzlingly
The sapphire walls of heaven.   The unsearch'd mine
Hath not such gems.   Earth's constellated thrones
Have not such pomp of purple and of gold.
It hath no features.   In its face is set
A mirror, and the gazer sees his own.
It looks a god, but it is like *himself !*
It hath a mien of empery, and smiles
Majestically sweet—but how like *him !*
It follows not with fortune.   It is seen
Rarely or never in the rich man's hall.

It seeks the chamber of the gifted boy,
And lifts his humble window, and comes in.
The narrow walls expand, and spread away
Into a kingly palace, and the roof
Lifts to the sky, and unseen fingers work
The ceilings with rich blazonry, and write
His name in burning letters over all.
And ever, as he shuts his wilder'd eyes,
The phantom comes and lays upon his lids
A spell that murders sleep, and in his ear
Whispers a deathless word, and on his brain
Breathes a fierce thirst no water will allay.
He is its slave henceforth! His days are spent
In chaining down his heart, and watching where
To rise by human weaknesses. His nights
Bring him no rest in all their blessed hours.
His kindred are forgotten or estranged.
Unhealthful fires burn constant in his eye.
His lip grows restless, and its smile is curl'd
Half into scorn—till the bright, fiery boy,
That was a daily blessing but to see,
His spirit was so bird-like and so pure,
Is frozen, in the very flush of youth,
Into a cold, care-fretted, heartless *man!*

   And what is its reward? At best a name!
Praise—when the ear has grown too dull to hear!
Gold—when the senses it should please are dead!
Wreaths—when the hair they cover has grown grey!
Fame—when the heart it should have thrill'd is numb!
All things but *love*—when love is all we want,
And close behind comes Death, and ere we know
That ev'n these unavailing gifts are ours,
He sends us, stripp'd and naked, to the grave!

.   .   .   .

Yet, oh ! what godlike gifts neglected lie
Wasting and marr'd in the forgotten soul !
The finest workmanship of God is there.
'Tis fleeter than the wings of light and wind ;
'Tis subtler than the rarest shape of air ;
Fire, and wind, and water do its will ;
Earth has no secret from its delicate eye—
The air no alchemy it solveth not ;
The star-writ heavens are read and understood,
And every sparry mineral hath a name,
And truth is recognised, and beauty felt,
And God's own image stamp'd upon its brow.

How is it so forgotten ?   *Will* it live
When the great firmament is roll'd away ?
Hath it a voice, for ever audible,
" I AM ETERNAL " ?   *Can* it overcome
This mocking passion-fiend, and even here
Live like a seraph upon truth and light ?

How can we ever be the slaves we are,
With a sweet angel sitting in our breasts !
How can we creep so lowly, when our wings
Tremble and plead for freedom !   Look at him
Who reads aright the image on his soul,
And gives it nurture like a child of light.
His life is calm and blessed, for his peace,
Like a rich pearl beyond the diver's ken,
Lies deep in his own bosom.   He is pure,
For the soul's errands are not done with men.
His senses are subdued and serve the soul.
He feels no void, for every faculty
Is used, and the fine balance of desire
Is perfect, and strains evenly, and on.
Content dwells with him, for his mind is fed,

And temperance has driven out unrest.
He heaps no gold.   It cannot buy him more
Of anything he needs.   The air of heaven
Visits no freshlier the rich man's brow ;
He has his portion of each silver star
Sent to his eye as freely, and the light
Of the blest sun pours on his book as clear
As on the golden missal of a king.
The spicy flowers are free to him ; the sward,
And tender moss, and matted forest leaves
Are as elastic to his weary feet ;
The pictures in the fountains, and beneath
The spreading trees, fine pencillings of light,
Stay while he gazes on them ; the bright birds
Know not that he is poor, and as he comes
From his low roof at morn, up goes the lark
Mounting and singing to the gate of heaven,
And merrily away the little brook
Trips with its feet of silver, and a voice
Almost articulate, of perfect joy.
Air to his forehead, water to his lips,
Heat to his blood, come just as faithfully,
And his own faculties as freely play.
Love fills his voice with music, and the tear
Springs at as light a bidding to his eye,
And his free limbs obey him, and his sight
Flies on its wondrous errands everywhere.
What does he need ?   Next to the works of God,
His friends are the rapt sages of old time.
And they impart their wisdom to his soul
In lavish fulness, when and where he will.
He sits in his mean dwelling, and communes
With Socrates and Plato, and the shades
Of all great men and holy, and the words
Written in fire by Milton, and the king

G

Of Israel, and the troop of glorious bards,
Ravish and steal his soul up to the sky—
And what is it to him, if these come in
And visit him, that at his humble door
There are no pillars with rich capitals,
And walls of curious workmanship within ?

———

THE ELMS OF NEW HAVEN.

[*Extracts from a Poem delivered before the Linonian Society of Yale
College, New Haven.*]

.   .   .   .

THE leaves we knew
Are gone these many summers, and the winds
Have scatter'd them all roughly through the world.
But still, in calm and venerable strength,
The old stems lift their burthens up to heaven,
And the young leaves, to the same pleasant tune,
Drink in the light, and strengthen, and grow fair.
The shadows have the same cool, emerald air ;
And prodigal as ever is the breeze,
Distributing the verdure's temperate balm.
The trees are sweet to us.   The outcry strong
Of the long-wandering and returning heart,
Is for the thing least changed.   A stone unturn'd
Is sweeter than a strange or alter'd face ;
A tree, that flings its shadows as of yore,
Will make the blood stir, sometimes, when the words
Of a long-look'd-for lip fall icy cold.
Ye, who in this Academy of shade,
Dreamt out the scholar's dream, and then away

On troubled seas went voyaging with Care,
But hail to-day the well-remember'd haven—
Ye, who at memory's trumpet-call, have stay'd
The struggling foot of life, the warring hand,
And, weary of the strife, come back to see
The green tent where your harness was put on—
Say—when you trod the shadowy street this morn,
Leapt not your heart up to the glorious trees?
Say—was it only to *my* sleep they came—
The angels, who to these remember'd trees
Brought me back, ever? I have come, in dream,
From many a far land, many a brighter sky,
And trod these dappled shadows till the morn.
From every Gothic aisle my heart fled home,
From every groinèd roof, and pointed arch,
To find its type in emerald beauty here.
The moon we worshipp'd thro' this trembling veil,
In other heavens seem'd garish and unclad.
The stars that burn'd to us thro' whispering leaves,
Stood cold and silently in other skies.
Stiller seem'd alway here the holy dawn
Hush'd by the breathless silence of the trees;
And who, that ever, on a Sabbath morn,
Sent thro' this leafy roof a prayer to heaven,
And when the sweet bells burst upon the air,
Saw the leaves quiver, and the flecks of light
Leap like caressing angels to the feet
Of the church-going multitude, but felt
That here, God's day was holier—that the trees,
Pierced by these shining spires, and echoing ever
"To prayer!" "To prayer!" were but the lofty roof
Of an unhewn cathedral, in whose choirs
Breezes and storm-winds, and the many birds
Join'd in the varied anthem; and that so,
Resting their breasts upon these bending limbs,

Closer, and readier to our need they lay—
The spirits who keep watch 'twixt us and heaven.

.   .   .   .

Alas! not spirits of bright wing alone
"Dwell by the oracle of God." The tree
That with its bright spray fans the sacred spire,
And trembles like a seraph's lyre to prayer,
Is peopled with the lying ministers
To new-born passions, who, with couchant ear,
Follow the lone steps of the musing boy,
And ere the wild wish struggles to the light,
Mask its dark features, and with silvery voice
Promise it wings resistless. Back, to-day,
Comes many a foot, all wearily and slow,
That went into the world with winged heel;
And many a man, still young, though wisely sad,
Paces the sweet old shadows with a sigh,
The spirits are so mute to manhood's ear
That tranced the boy with music. On a night,
The fairest of a summer, years ago,
There walk'd a youth beneath these arching trees.
The moon was in mid-heaven, an orb of gold.
The air was rock'd asleep, or, 'mid the leaves
Walked without whisper. On the pavement lay
The broken moonbeams, like a silver net,
Massive and motionless, and, if a bird
Sang a half carol as the moon wore on
And look'd into his nest, or if the note
Of a monotonous insect caught the ear,
The silence was but challenged by the sound,
And night seem'd stiller after. With his heart
Robb'd of its sentinel, the youth paced on.
His truant soul lay breathless on his lips,
Drowsed with the spell of the voluptuous air;

And shut was memory's monitory book;
And mute, alas! as they will sometimes be,
Were heaven's rebuking angels.   Then uprose,
In the unguarded chamber of his heart,
A murmur, inarticulate and wild;
And ere it had a semblance, or a name,
A soft voice from the trees said, " Wak'st thou there?
Wak'st thou at last, O nature?   Thou hast slept
Far through the morn, and glowing flowers of ear,
Many and bright ones, hast thou lost for ever!
But life is full of roses—come away!
Shut up those dreary books, and come away!
Why is the night so passionately sweet,
If made for study and a brow of care?
Why are your lips pride, and your eyes soft fire?—
Why beautiful in youth,—if cold to joy?
List to the pleading senses, where they lie,
Numb and forgotten in the cell of thought;
Yet are they God's gift—precious as the rest.
Use what thou hast—turn to the soft path ever,—
And, in the garden of this pleasant world,
Pluck what seems fairest to thee!"   A light wind
Stole through the trees, and with its airy hand
Lifted the leafy veil from off the moon;
And steadfastly Night's solemn eye look'd in
Upon the flush'd face of the troubled boy—
And the mysterious voice was heard no more.

Again 'twas night.   A storm was in the air;
And, by his pale and solitary lamp,
A youth of sterner temper than the last,
Kept the lone scholar's vigil.   He had laid
His book upon its face, and with his head
Turn'd to the rattling casement, sat erect,
And listen'd to the shrill, tempestuous wind.

Gust after gust swept by, and as the scream
Of the careering tempest fiercer came,
The youth's dark brow crouch'd lowering to his eye,
And his thin lips press'd bloodlessly together;
And with some muttering words, as if replying
To voices that call'd to him from the storm,
He rose, and hurriedly strode forth. The air
Below the lashing tree-tops was all black.
The lofty trunks creak'd staggering in the wind,
But all invisibly; and in the sky
Was only so much light as must be there
While hope is in the world. Small need had then
The spirit who would wile that heart from heaven
To lend it mask or utterance. With step
Reckless and fast the wanderer sped on,
And as the tempest smote upon his breast,
And howlingly fled past, he clench'd his hands,
And struck his strong arms thro' the air, and rush'd
Headlong with flying fury thro' the dark.
Breathless and hoarse, at last, against the trunk
Of a vast tree he stood; and to an ear
Bending from out the branches as they swung,
Unconsciously he mutter'd:—"I am weak,
And this wild storm is mighty; but I feel
A joy in its career, as if my soul
Breathed only thus. I am aroused—unchain'd,
Something gives outcry in me that was dumb,
Something that pined for weapons is in arms,
And set on with a trumpet. Glorious blast!
What is my poor tranquillity of life—
My abject study—to thy storming joy?
An intellect is mine—a passive soul
Antagonist to nothing—while for thee,
A senseless element, are wings and power—
Power to dash the stars out from the sky—

Wings to keep pace with midnight round the world.
The lightning's fiery traverse is no bar,
The thunder's hush no check, the howling trees
Only thy music.   Demon, if thou art !
Prince of the powers of air, if such there be !
Darkness and conflict are my element,
As they are thine !"   The storm lull'd suddenly,
The tortured trees stood silent in the gloom,
And all was still—save that amid the leaves
Stirr'd a low murmur, which, like airy lips,
Whispering close into the scholar's ear,
Became articulate :—" Be calm ! be calm !
Return to thy neglected books, and read !
Thou shalt have all thou wilt, but, in thy books,
Lie weapons keener than the lightning's edge,
And in thy intellect a power of ill
To which the storm-wind is an infant's anger.
The blast blots out the stars that shine again,
The storm-wind and the darkness leave the trees
Brighter for morn to smile on ; but the mind
Forges from knowledge an archangel's spear,
And, with the spirits that compel the world,
Conflicts for empire.   Call thy hate of day,
Thy scorn of men, *ambition !*—and, if moved
By something in thy heart to wrong and slay —
Justice sits careless with a bloody sword ;
Religion has remorseless whips ; and gold
Brings to thy spurning foot the necks of men.
Be *thou* the sword—the whip—get thou the gold—
And borne triumphant upon human praise,
The lightning were too slow to do thy will—
The stormy night not black enough."   Again
Toward the window glimmering thro' the dark
The scholar turn'd, and with a pallid brow,
But lips of marble, fed his wasting lamp,

And patiently read down the morning star.
And he was changed thenceforward.

.   .   .   .

                              Wave once more
The wand athwart the mirror of the past.
A summer's eve in June.   The sun had shot
A golden arrow down yon leafy aisle,
And to his tent gone in.   The dusty air
Paraded in his glory.   The bright spires,
Like mourners who still see the lost in heaven,
Shone in his smile as if he had not set;
And presently, amid his glowing track,
Like one who came reluctant to replace
The great light newly fled, the evening star
Stood forth with timid and diminish'd ray—
But brighten'd as the sun was longer gone.
Life was a feast at this delicious hour,
And all came forth to it.   The bent old man
Paced musingly before his open door.
The tired child, with hands cross'd droopingly,
Sat at the threshold.   Slowly pass'd the dame ;
Slowly the listless scholar, sauntering back
To his shut books unwillingly ; and low—
Soften'd and low—as if the chord of love
Were struck and harmonised throughout the world,
The hum of voices rose upon the air.
Hush'd were the trees the while ; and voiceless lay
The wakeful spirits in the leaves, till, lo !
A pale youth,* mingling in the throng !   With light
And airy step, and mien of such a grace
As breathes thro' marble from the sculptor's dream,
He pass'd, and after him the stranger's eye
Turn'd with inquiring wonder.   Dumb no more

* James Hillhouse, who had died at New Haven a few months before.

Were the invisible dwellers in the trees;
For, as he went, the feathery branches seem'd
To "syllable his name;" and to the ears
Of them who met him, whispering music flew,
Stealing their hearts away to link to his.
" Love him!" the old man heard as if the leaves
Of his own roof-tree murmur'd it; "Love well
The poet who may sow your grave with flowers,
The traveller to the far land of the Past,
Lost to your feet for ever!" Sadly lean'd
The mourner at her window as he came,
And the far-drooping elm-leaf touch'd her brow,
And whisper'd, "*He* has counted all thy tears!
The breaking chord was audible to him!
The agony for which thou, weeping, saidst
There was no pity, for its throbs were dumb—
He look'd but in thine eyes, and read it all!
Love him, for sorrowing with thee!" The sad child,
Sitting alone with his unheeded grief,
Look'd at him through his tears, and smiled to hear
The same strange voice that talk'd to him in dreams
Speak from the low tree softly; and it said—
"The stranger who looks on thee loves the child!
He has seen angels like thee; and thy sorrow
Touches his own, as he goes silent by.
Love him, fair child!" The poor man, from his door,
Look'd forth with cheerful face, and as the eye,
The soft eye of the poet, turn'd to his,
A whisper from the tree said, "This is he
Who knows thy heart is human as his own,
Who, with inspirèd numbers, tells the world
That love dwells with the lowly. He has made
The humble roof a burthen in sweet song—
Interpreted thy heart to happier men!
Love him! oh, love him, therefore!" The stern man,

Who, with the tender spirit of a child,
Walks in some thorny path, unloved and lone ;
The maiden with her secret ; the sad mother,
Speaking no more of her dishonour'd boy,
But bound to him with all her heart-strings yet, —
These heard the trees say, as the poet pass'd,
" Yours is the mournful poetry of life,
And in the sad lines of your silent lips,
Reads he with tenderest pity !   Knit to him
The hearts he opens like a claspèd book,
And, in the honey'd music of his verse,
Hear your dumb griefs made eloquent ! "   With eye
Watchful and moist, the poet kept his way,
Unconscious of the love around him springing ;
And when from its bent path the evening star
Stepp'd silently, and left the lesser fires
Lonely in heaven, the poet had gone in,
Mute with the many sorrows he had seen ;
And, with the constancy of starry eyes,
The hearts he touch'd drew to him.

———

THE BURIAL OF THE CHAMPION OF HIS CLASS, AT YALE COLLEGE.

Ye've gather'd to your place of prayer
   With slow and measur'd tread :
Your ranks are full, your mates all there—
   But the soul of one has fled.
He was the proudest in his strength,
   The manliest of ye all ;
Why lies he at that fearful length,
   And ye around his pall ?

Ye reckon it in days, since he
  Strode up that foot-worn aisle,
With his dark eye flashing gloriously,
  And his lip wreathed with a smile.
Oh, had it been but told you, then,
  To mark whose lamp was dim—
From out yon rank of fresh-lipp'd men,
  Would ye have singled him?

Whose was the sinewy arm, that flung
  Defiance to the ring?
Whose laugh of victory loudest rung—
  Yet not for glorying?
Whose heart, in generous deed and thought,
  No rivalry might brook,
And yet distinction claiming not?
  There lies he—go and look!

On now—his requiem is done,
  The last deep prayer is said—
On to his burial, comrades—on,
  With the noblest of the dead!
Slow—for it presses heavily—
  It is a man ye bear!
Slow, for our thoughts dwell wearily
  On the noble sleeper there.

Tread lightly, comrades!—we have laid
  His dark locks on his brow—
Like life—save deeper light and shade:
  We'll not disturb them now.
Tread lightly—for 'tis beautiful,
  That blue-vein'd eyelid's sleep,
Hiding the eye death left so dull—
  Its slumber we will keep.

Rest now ! his journeying is done—
    Your feet are on his sod—
Death's chain is on your champion—
    He waiteth here his God.
Ay, turn and weep ; 'tis manliness
    To be heart-broken here—
For the grave of earth's best nobleness
    Is water'd by the tear.

———

THE LADY JANE.

A HUMOROUS NOVEL IN RHYME.

I.

THERE was a lady—fair, and forty too.
    There was a youth of scarcely two-and-twenty.
The story of their loves is strange, yet true.
    I'll tell it you !   Romances are so plenty
In prose, that you'll be glad of something new.
    And so (in rhyme) for " what the devil meant he ! "
You think he was too young !—but tell me whether
The moth and humming-bird grow old together !

II.

Nature, that made the ivy-leaf and lily,
    Not of *one* warp and woof hath made us all !
Bent goes the careful, and erect the silly,
    And wear and tear makes difference—not small ;

And he that hath no money—will-he, nill-he—
    Is thrust like an old man against the wall !
Grief out of some the very life-blood washes ;
Some shed it like ducks' backs and " Mackintoshes."

III.

The Lady Jane was daughter of an Earl—
    Shut from approach like sea-nymph in her shell,
Never a rude breath stirr'd the floating curl
    Upon her marble temple, and naught fell
Upon the ear of the patrician girl
    But pride-check'd syllables, all measured well.
Her suitors were her father's and not hers—
So were her debts at " Storr and Mortimer's."

IV.

Her health was lady-like.   No blood, in riot,
    Tangled the tracery of her veined cheek,
Nor seem'd her exquisite repose the quiet
    Of one by suffering made sweet and meek.
She ate and drank, and probably lived by it,
    And liked her cup of tea by no means weak !
Untroubled by debt, lovers, or affliction,
Her pulse beat with extremely little friction.

V.

Yet was there fire within her soft grey eye,
    And room for pressure on her lip of rose ;
And few who saw her gracefully move by,
    Imagined that her feelings slept, or froze.

You may have seen the cunning florist tie
   A thread about a bud, which never blows,
But, with shut chalice from the sun and rain,
Hoards up the morn—and such the Lady Jane.

VI.

The old lord had had offers for her hand,
   The which he answer'd—by his secretary.
And, doubtless, some were for the lady's land,
   The men being old and valetudinary;
But there were others who were all unmann'd,
   And fell into a life of wild vagary,
In their despair. To tell his daughter of it,
The cold Earl thought would be but little profit.

VII.

And so she bloom'd—all fenced around with care;
   And none could find a way to win or woo her.
When visible at home—the Earl was there!
   Abroad—her chaperon stuck closely to her!
She was a sort of nun in open air,
   Known to but few, and intimate to fewer:
And, always used to conversation guarded,
She thought all men talked just as her papa did.

VIII.

Pause while you read, O Broadway demoiselle!
   And bless your stars that long before *you* marry,
You are a judge of passion pleaded well!
   For you have listen'd to Tom, Dick, and Harry,

And, if kind Heaven endowed you for a belle,
   At least your destiny did not miscarry !
"You've had your fling"—and now all wise and steady,
For matrimony's cares you're cool and ready !

IX.

And yet the bloom upon the fruit is fair !
   And "ignorance *is* bliss " in teaching love !
And guarding lips, when others have been there,
   Is apt uneasy reveries to move !
I really think mammas should have a care !
   And though of nunneries I disapprove,
'Tis easier to make blushes hear to reason
Than to unteach a "Saratoga Season."

X.

In France, where, it is said, they wiser are,
   Miss may not walk out, even with her cousin ;
And when she is abroad from bolt and bar,
   A well-bred man should be to her quite frozen ;
And so at last, like a high-priced attar
   Hermetically seal'd in silk and resin,
She is delivered safe to him who loves her ;
And then—with whom she will she's hand and glove, sir !

XI.

I know this does not work well, and that ours
   Are the best wives on earth.   They love their spouses,
Who prize them—as you do centennial flowers,
   For having bloom'd, though not in *your* greenhouses.

'Tis a bold wooer that dare talk of dowers.
    And where *I* live, the milking of the cows is
Too rude a task for females! Well. 'Twould hurt you,
Where women are so prized, to sneer at virtue.

XII.

" Free-born Americans," they must have freedom!
    They'll stay—if they have leave to run away.
They're ministering angels when you need 'em,
    But 'specially want credit in Broadway.
French wives are more particular how you feed 'em,
    The English drag you oftener to the play.
But ours we quite enslave—(more true than funny)—
With " heaven-born liberty," and *trust*—or money!

XIII.

Upon her *thirtieth* birthday, Lady Jane
    Thought sadly on the *twenties!* Even the *'teens,*
That she had said farewell to, without pain—
    Leaves falling from a flower that nothing means—
Seem'd worth regathering to live again;
    But not like Ruth, fares Memory, who gleans
After the careful Harvester of years :—
The Lady Jane thought on't with bitter tears!

XIV.

She glided to her mirror. From the air
    Glided to meet her, with its tearful eyes,
A semblance sad, but beautifully fair;
    And gradually there stole a sweet surprise

Under her lids, and as she laid the hair
  Back from her snowy brow, Madonna-wise,
"Time, after all," she said, " a harmless flirt is ! "
And from that hour took kindly to her *thirties*.

XV.

And, with his honours not at all unsteady,
  The Decimal elect stepp'd coolly in ;
And having all his nights and mornings ready,
  He'd very little trouble to begin.
And *Twenty* was quite popular,—they said he
  Went out of office with so little din !
The old Earl did not celebrate (nor ought he)
Her birthdays more.   And like a dream came *Forty*.

XVI.

And on the morn of it she stood to dress,
  Mock'd by that flattering semblance, as before,
And lifted with a smile the raven tress,
  That, darkening her white shoulder, swept the floor.
Time had not touch'd her dazzling loveliness !
  " Yet is it time," she said, " that I give o'er—
I'm an old maid !—and though I suffer by it, I
Must change my style and leave off gay society."

XVII.

And so she did.   Her maid by her desire
  Comb'd her luxuriant locks behind her ears ;
She had her dresses alter'd to come higher,
  Though it dissolved the dressmaker in tears !

H

And flung a new French hat into the fire,
    Which she had bought, "forgetful of her years."
This t' anticipate "the world's dread laugh!"
Most persons think too much of it, by half.

XVIII.

I do not mean to say that generally
    The "virtuous single" take too soon to tea;
But now and then you find one who could rally
    At forty, and go back to twenty-three—
A handsome, plump, affectionate "Aunt Sally,"
    With no taste for cats, flannel, and Bohea!
And I would have her, spite of "he or she says,"
Up heart, and pin her kerchief as she pleases.

XIX.

Some men, 'tis said, prefer a woman fat—
    Lord Byron did.   Some like her very spare.
Some like a lameness.   (I have known one that
    Would go quite far enough for your despair,
And *halt* in time.)   Some like them delicate
    As lilies, and with some "the only wear"
Is one whose sex has spoil'd a midshipman.
Some only like what pleased another man.

XX.

I like one that *likes me*.   But there's a kind
    Of women, very dangerous to poets,
Whose hearts beat with a truth that seems like mind—
    A nature that, though passionate, will show its

Devotion by not being rash or blind ;
  But by sweet study grows to love.   And so it's
Not odd if they are counted cold, though handsome,
And never meet a man who understands 'em.

XXI.

By *never*, I mean late in life.   But ah !
  How exquisite their love and friendship then !
Perennial of soul such women are,
  And readers of the hearts of gifted men ;
And as the deep well mourns the hidden star,
  And mirrors the first ray that beams again,
They—be the loved light lost or dimly burning,
Feel all its clouds, and trust its bright returning.

XXII.

In outward seeming tranquil and subdued,
  Their hearts beneath beat youthfully and fast.
Time and imprison'd love make not a prude ;
  And warm the gift we know to be the last ;
And pure is the devotion that must brood
  Upon *your* hopes alone—for *hers* are past !
Trust me, " a rising man " rose seldom higher,
But some dear, sweet old maid has pull'd the wire.

XXIII.

The Lady Jane, (pray do not think that hers
  Was quite the character I've drawn above.
Old maids, like young, have various calibres,
  And hers was moderate, though she was " a love,")

The Lady Jane call'd on the dowagers—
    Mainly her slight acquaintance to improve,
But partly with a docile wish to know
What solaces of age were *comme il faut.*

XXIV.

They stared at her plain hat and air demure,
    But answer'd her with some particularity ;
And she was edified you may be sure,
    And added vastly to her popularity.
She found a dozen mad on furniture,
    Five on embroidery, and none on charity ;
But her last call—the others were but short ones—
Turn'd out to Lady Jane of some importance.

XXV.

The door was open'd by a Spanish page—
    A handsome lad in green with bullet buttons,
Who look'd out like a trulian from a cage,
    And deign'd to glance at the tall menial but once,
Then bent, with earnestness beyond his age,
    His eyes, (you would have liked to see them shut once,
The fringes were so long)—on Lady Jane.
The varlet clearly thought her not so plain.

XXVI.

And bounding up the flower-laden stair,
    He waited her ascent, then open flung
A mirror, clear as 'twere a door of air,
    Which on its silver hinge with music swung—

Contrived that never foot should enter there
  Unheralded by that melodious tongue.
This delicate alarum is worth while
More 'specially with carpets of three-pile.

XXVII.

Beyond a gallery extended, cool,
  And softly lighted, and, from dome to floor,
Hung pictures—mostly the Venetian school;
  Each " worth a Jew's eye "—very likely more ;
And drapery, gold-broider'd in Stamboul,
  Closed the extremity in lieu of door :
This the page lifted, and disclosed to view
The boudoir of the Countess Pasibleu.

XXVIII.

It was a small pavilion lined with pink,—
  Mirrors and silk all, save the door and skylight,
The latter of stain'd glass.   (You would not think
  How juvenescent is a rosy high light !)
Upon the table were seen pen and ink,
  (Two things I cannot say have stood in *my* light,)
Amid a host of trinkets, toys, and fans ;
The table in the style of Louis Quinze.

XXIX.

A singular and fragile little creature
  Upon the cushions indolently lay,
With waning life in each transparent feature,
  But youth in her bright lips' ethereal play ;

In short, the kind of creature that would meet your
    Conception of a transmigrating fay—
The dark eyes, not at all worn-out or weary,
Kindling for transfer to some baby Peri!

XXX.

The rest used up, past mending.   Yet her tones
    Were wildly, deeply, exquisitely clear;
Though voice is not a thing of flesh and bones,
    And probably goes *up* when they stay *here*.
(I do not know how much of Smith and Jones
    Will bear translating to " the better sphere,")
But ladies, certainly, when they shall climb to't,
Will get their dimples back—tho' not the rhyme to't.

XXXI.

Her person was dress'd very like her soul—
    In fine material most loosely worn.
A cobweb cashmere struggled to control
    Ringlets that laugh'd the filmy folds to scorn,
And, from the shawls in which she nestled, stole
    The smallest slipper ever soil'd or torn.
You would not guess her age by looking at her,
Nor from my sketch, of course.   We'll leave that matter.

XXXII.

" My dear ! " the Countess said, (by this time she
    Had ceased the Weather, poor old man, to hammer—
He gets it in these morning calls, *pardie!*
    And Lady Jane had hinted with a stammer

Her errand—somewhat delicate, you see,)
    " My dear, how very odd ! I fear I am a
Poor judge of age—(who made that funny bonnet ?)
Indeed, I always turn'd my back upon it !

XXXIII.

"Time has no business in one's house, my dear !
    I'm not at home to any of my creditors.
They send their nasty bills in, once a year,
    And Time's are like Mortality's—mere '*dead* letters.'
Besides, what comfort is there living here,
    If every stupid hour's to throw Death's head at us ?
(Lend me a pin, dear !)   Time at last will stop us :
But, come to that—we're free by *habeas corpus.*

XXXIV.

("Fie, what a naughty shawl !   No *exposé*,
    I trust, love, eh ?   Hold there, thou virtuous pin !)
And so you really have come out to-day
    To look you up some suitable new sin ! "
"Oh, Countess ! "   "Did you never write a play ?
    Nor novel ?   Well, you really should begin !
For, (hark, my dear !) the publishers are biters,
Not the book's fine *title*—but the writer's.

XXXV.

" You're half an authoress ; for, as my maid says,
    ' Begun's half done,' and you've your *title* writ.
I quote from Colburn, and as what ' the trade ' says
    Is paid for, it is well consider'd wit.

Genius, undoubtedly, of many grades is,
    But as to us, we do not need a bit.
'Three volumes,' says the bargain, 'not too thin.'
You don't suppose I'd throw him genius in!"

XXXVI.

" But *fame*, dear Countess!" At the word there flush'd
    A colour to her cheek like fever's glow,
And in her hand unconsciously she crush'd
    The fringes of her shawl, and bending low
To hide the tears that suddenly had gush'd
    Into her large, dark eyes, she murmur'd "No!
Th' inglorious agony of conquering pain
Has drunk that dream up.   I have lived in vain!

XXXVII.

" Yet have I set my soul upon the string,
    Tense with the energy of high desire,
And trembled with the arrow's quivering spring,
    To launch upon ambition's flight of fire!
And never lark so hush'd his heart to sing,
    Or, as he sang, nerved wing to bear it higher
As I have striven my wild heart to tame
And melt its love, pride, passion—into fame!

XXXVIII.

" Oh, poor the flattery to call it mine
    For trifles which beguiled an hour of pain,
Or, on the echoing heels of mirth and wine,
    Crept through the chambers of a throbbing brain.

Worthily, have I never written line !
  And when they talk to me of *fame* I gain,
In very bitterness of soul I mock it,—
  And put the net proceeds into my pocket !

XXXIX.

" And so, my dear,—let not the market vary,—
  I bid the critics, *pro* and *con*, defiance ;
And then I'm fond of being literary,
  And have a tenderness for ' sucking lions.'
My friend the Duchess has a fancy dairy :—
  Cheeses or poets, curds or men of science—
It comes to the same thing. But, truce to mocking—
Suppose you try my colour in a stocking ?"

XL.

I need not state the ratiocination
  By which the Lady Jane had so decided—
Not quite upon the regular vocation—
  Of course you know she was too rich (or *I* did)
To care with Costard for " remuneration ;"
  But feeling that her life like Lethe glided,
She thought 'twould be advisable to bag her a
Few brace of rapids from her friend's Niagara.

XLI.

" Well, Countess ! what shall be my *premier pas ?*
  Must I propitiate the penny-a-liners ?
Or would a ' sucking lion' stoop so far
  As to be fed and petted by a dry nurse ?

I cannot shine—but I can *see* a star—
    Are there not worshippers as well as shiners?
I will be ruled implicitly by you :—
My stocking's innocent—how dye it *blue ?* "

XLII.

The Countess number'd on her fingers, musing :—
    " I've several that I might make you over,
And not be inconsolable at losing ;
    But, really, as you've neither spouse nor lover,
'Most any of my pets would be amusing,
    Particularly if you're not above a
Discreet flirtation.   Are you?   How's the Earl?
Does he still treat you like a little girl?

XLIII.

" How do you see your visitors?   Alone?
    Does the Earl sleep at table after dinner?
Have you had many lovers?   Dear me!   None?
    Was not your father something of a sinner?
Who is the nicest man you've ever known?
    Pray, does the butler bring your letters in, or
First take them to the Earl?   Is he not rather
A surly dog?—the butler, not your father."

XLIV.

To these inquiries the Lady Jane
    Replied with nods, or something as laconic,
For on the Countess rattled, might and main,
    With a rapidity Napoleonic ;

Then mused and said, " 'Twill never do, it's plain—
  The poet must be warranted Platonic !
But, query—how to find you such an oddity ?
My dear, they *all* make love !—it's their commodity !

XLV.

" The poet's on the look-out for a scene—
  The painter for a ' novel situation ;'
And either does much business between
  The little pauses of a declaration—
Noting the way in which you sob or lean,
  Or use your handkerchief in agitation.
I've known one—making love like Roderick Random—
Get off his knees and make a memorandum !

XLVI.

" You see they're always ready for the trade,
  And have a speech as pat as a town-crier ;
And so, my dear, I'm naturally afraid
  To trust you with these gentlemen-on-fire.
I knew a most respectable old maid
  A dramatist made love to—just to try her !
She hung herself, of course—but in that way
He got some pretty touches for his play.

XLVII.

" How shall we manage it ?   I say, with tears,
  I've only two that are not rogues at bottom ;
And one of those would soon be ' over ears '
  In love with you,—but that he hasn't got 'em.

They were cut off by the New Zealanders—
    (As he invariably adds) ''od-rot-'em!'
(Meaning the savages.)   He's quite a poet,
(He wears his hair so that you wouldn't know it,)

XLVIII.

" In his ideas, I mean.   (I really *am* at a
    Stand-still about you.)   Well—this man, one day,
Took in his head to own the earth's diameter,
    From *zenith* through to *nadir!*   (They *do* say
He kill'd his wife—or threw a ham at her—
    Or something—so he had to go away—
That's neither here nor there.)   His name is Wieland,
And under him exactly lies New Zealand.

XLIX.

" I'm not certain if his ' seat ' 's, or no,
    In the Low Countries.   But the sky above it
Of course is his ; and for some way below
    He has a right to dig and to improve it ;
But under him, a million miles or so,
    Lies land that's *not* his,—and the law can't move it.
It cut poor Wieland's *nadir* off, no doubt—
And so he sail'd to buy the owner out.

L.

" I never quite made out the calculation—
    But plump against his cellar floor, bin 2,
He found a tribe had built their habitation,
    Whose food was foreigners and kangaroo.

They would sell out—but, to his consternation,
  They charged him—all the fattest of his crew !
At last they caught and roasted every one—
But he escaped by being under-done ! "

LI.

That such a lion was well worth his feed,
  Confess'd with merry tears the Lady Jane ;
But, that he answer'd to her present need,
  (A literary pet,) was not so plain.
She thought she'd give the matter up, indeed,
  Or turn it over and so call again.
However, as her friend had mention'd two,
Perhaps the other might be made to do.

LII.

" I'm looking," said the Countess, " for a letter
  From my old playmate, Isabella Gray.
'Tis Heaven knows how long since I have met her !
  She ran away and married one fine day—
Poor girl !   She might have done a great deal better !
  The boy that she has sent to me, they say,
Is handsome, and has talents very striking :
So young, too—you can spoil him to your liking.

LIII.

" Her letter will amuse you.   You must know
  That, from her marriage-day, her lord has shut her
Securely up in an old French chateau ;
  Where, with her children and no woman but her,

He plays the old-school gentleman ; and so
   Her worldly knowledge stopp'd at bread and butter.
She thinks I may be changed by time—for, may be,
I've lost a tooth or got another baby.

LIV.

" Heigh-ho !—'tis evident we're made of clay,
   And harden unless kept in tears and shade ;
This fashionable sunshine dries away
   Much that we err in losing, I'm afraid !
I wonder what my guardian angels say
   About the sort of woman I have made !
I wish I could begin my life again !
What think you of Pythagoras, Lady Jane ?"

LV.

The Countess, all this while, was running over
   The pages of a letter, closely cross'd :—
" I wish," she said, " my most devoted lover
   Took half the trouble that this scrawl has cost !
Though some of it is quite a flight above a
   Sane woman's comprehension. Tut ! Where was't !
There is a passage here—the name's Beaulevres—
His chateau's in the neighbourhood of Sevres.

LVI.

" The boy's call'd Jules. Ah, here it is ! *My child*
   Brings you this letter. I've not much to say
More than you know of him, if he has smiled
   When you have seen him. In his features play

The light from which his soul has been beguiled—
The blessed heaven I lose with him to-day.
I ask you not to love him—he is there !
And you have loved him—without wish or prayer !

LVII.

His father sends him forth for fame and go'd —
An angel on this errand !   I have striven
Against it—but he is not mine to hold.
They say 'tis wrong to wish to stay him, even,
And that my pride's poor—my ambition cold !
Alas ! to get him only back to heaven
Is my one passionate prayer !   Think me not wild—
'Tis that I have an angel for my child !

LVIII.

They say that he has genius.   I but see
That he gets wisdom as the flower gets hue,
While others hive it like the toiling bee ;
That, with him, all things beautiful keep new,
And every morn the first morn seems to be—
So freshly look abroad his eyes of blue !
What he has written seems to me no more
Than I have thought a thousand times before !

LIX.

Yet not upon his gay career to Fame
Broods my foreboding tear.   I wish it won—
My prayer speeds on his spirit to its aim—
But in his chamber wait I for my son !

When darken'd is ambition's star of fame—
   When the night's fever of unrest is on—
With the unbidden sadness, the sharp care,
I fly from his bright hours, to meet him there!

LX.

Forgive me if I prate!   Is't much—is't wild—
   To hope—to pray—that you will sometimes creep
To the dream-haunted pillow of my child,
   Keeping sweet watch above his fitful sleep?
Blest like his mother, if in dream he smiled,
   Or, if he wept, still blest with him to weep;
Rewarded—oh, for how much more than this!—
By his awaking smile—his morning kiss!

LXI.

I know not how to stop!   He leaves me well;
   Life, spirit, health, in all his features speak;
His foot bounds with the spring of a gazelle;
   But watch him—stay! well thought on!—there's a streak
Which the first faltering of his tongue will tell,
   Long ere the bright blood wavers on his cheek—
A little bursted vein, that, near his heart,
Looks like a crimson thread half torn apart.

LXII.

So, trusting not his cheek by morning light,
   When hope sits mantling on it, seek his bed
In the more tranquil watches of the night,
   And ask this tell-tale how his heart has sped.

If well—its branching tracery shows bright ;
  But if its sanguine hue look cold and dead,
Ah, Gertrude ! let your ministering be
As you would answer it, in heaven, to me ! "

LXIII.

Enter the page :—" Miladi's maid is waiting !"—
  A hint (that it was time to dress for dinner,)
Which puts a stop in London to all prating.
  As far as goes the letter you're a winner,
The rest of it to flannel shirts relating—
  When Jules should wear his thicker, when his thinner.
The Countess laugh'd at Lady Jane's adieu :
She thought the letter touching.   Pray, don't you ?

LXIV.

I have observed that Heaven, in answering prayer,
  (This is not meant to be a pious stanza—
Only a fact that has a pious air.)
  (We're very sure, I think, to have an answer ;)
But I've observed, I would remark, that where
  Our plans are ill-contrived, as oft our plans are,
Kind Providence goes quite another way
To bring about the end for which we pray.

LXV.

In this connection I would also add,
  That a discreet young angel (*bonâ fide*),
Accompanied our amiable lad ;
  And that he walk'd not out, nor stepp'd aside he,

I

Nor met with an adventure, good or bad,
   (Although he enter'd London on a Friday,)
Nor ate, nor drank, nor closed his eye a minute,
Without this angel's guiding finger in it.

LXVI.

His mother, as her letter seems to show,
   Expected him, without delay or bother,—
Portmanteau, carpet-bag, and all—to go
 Straight to her old friend's house—forsooth! what other!
The angel, who would seem the world to know,
   Advised the boy to drive to Mivart's rather.
He did.   The angel, (as I trust is plain,)
Lodged in the vacant heart of Lady Jane.

LXVII.

A month in town these gentlemen had been
   At date of the commencement of my story.
The angel's occupations you have seen,
   If you have read what I have laid before ye.
Jules had seen Dan O'Connell and the Queen,
   And girded up his loins for fame and glory,
And changed his old integuments for better ;
And then he call'd and left his mother's letter.

LXVIII.

That female hearts grow never old in towns—
   That taste grows rather young with dissipation—
That dowagers dress not in high-neck'd gowns—
   Nor are, at fifty, proof against flirtation—

That hospitality is left to clowns,
 Or elbow'd from the world by ostentation—
That a "tried friend" should not be tried again—
That boys at seventeen are partly men—

LXIX.

Are truths, as pat as paving-stones, in cities.
 The contrary is true of country air;
(Where the mind rusts, which is a thousand pities,
 While still the cheek keeps fresh and debonnair.)
But what I'm trying in this verse to hit is,
 That Heaven, in answering Jules's mother's prayer,
Began by thwarting all her plans and suavities;
As needs must—*vide* the just-named depravities.

LXX.

Some stanzas back, we left the ladies going,
 At six, to dress for dinner. Time to dine
I always give in poetry, well knowing
 That, to jump over it in half a line,
Looks (let us be sincere, dear muse!) like showing
 Contempt we *do not* feel, for meat and wine.
Dinner! Ye Gods! What is there more respectable!
For eating, who, save Byron, ever check'd a belle!

LXXI.

'Tis ten—say half-past. Lady Jane has dined,
 And dress'd as simply as a lady may.
A card lies on her table "To Remind"—
 'Tis odd she never thought of it to-day.

But she is pleasantly surprised to find
   'Tis Friday night, the Countess's *soirée*.
Back rolls the chariot to Berkeley Square.
If you have dined, dear reader, let's go there !

LXXII.

We're early. In the cloak-room smokes the urn,
   The housekeeper behind it, fat and solemn :
Steady as stars the fresh-lit candles burn,
   And on the stairs the new-blown what d'ye-call-'em
Their nodding cups of perfume overturn ;
   The page leans idly by a marble column,
And stiffly a tall footman stands above,
Looking between the fingers of his glove.

LXXIII.

All bright and silent, like a charmèd palace—
   The spells wound up, the fays to come at twelve ;
The housekeeper a witch, (*cum grano salis ;*)
   The handsome page, perhaps, a royal elve
Condemn'd to servitude by fairy malice ;
   (I wish the varlet had these rhymes to delve !)
Some magic hall, it seems, for revel bright,
And Lady Jane the spirit first alight.

LXXIV.

Alas ! here vanishes the foot of Pleasure !
   She—like an early guest—goes in before,
And comes, when all are gone, for Memory's treasure ;
   But is not found upon the crowded floor ;

(Unless, indeed, some charming woman says you're
  A love, which makes close quarters less a bore.)
I've seen her, down Anticipation's vista,
As large as life—and walk'd straight on, and miss'd her !

LXXV.

With a declining taste for making friends,
  One's taste for the fatigue of pleasure's past ;
And then, one sometimes wonders which transcends—
  The first hour of a gay night, or the last.
(Beginners " burn the candle at both ends,"
  And find the *middle* brightest—*that* is fast !)
But a good rule at parties, (to keep up a
Mercurial air,) is to *come in at supper.*

LXXVI.

I mean that you should go to bed at nine
  And sleep till twelve—take coffee or green tea,
Dress and go out—(this was a way of mine
  When looking up the world in '33)—
Sup at the ball—(it's not a place for wine)—
  Sleep, or not, after, as the case may be.
You've the advantage, thus, when all are yawning,
Of growing rather fresher toward morning.

LXXVII.

But, after thirty, *here's* your best " Elixir : "
  Breakfast betimes. Do something worth your while
By twelve or one (this makes the blood run quick, sir !)
  Dine with some man or woman *who will smile.*

Have little cause to care how politics are,
　　"Let not the sun go down upon your" bile;
And, if well-married, rich, and not too clever,
I don't see why you shouldn't live for ever.

LXXVIII.

Short-lived is your "sad dog"—and yet, we hear,
　　"Whom the gods love die young." Of course the ladies
Are safe in loving what the gods hold dear;
　　And the result, I'm very much afraid, is,
That if he "has his day," it's "neither here
　　Nor there!" But it is time our hero made his
Appearance on the carpet, Lady Jane—
(I'll mend this vile pen, and begin again.)

LXXIX.

The Lady Jane walk'd thro' the bright rooms, breaking
　　The glittering silence with her flowing dress,
Whose pure folds seem'd a coy resistance making
　　To the fond air; while, to her loveliness
The quick-eyed mirrors breathlessly awaking,
　　Acknowledged not one radiant line the less
That not on *them* she look'd before she faded!
Neglected gentlemen don't do as they did:—

LXXX.

No!—for, 'twixt *our* quicksilver and a woman,
　　Nature has put no glass, for non-conductor,
And, while she's imaged in their bosoms, few men
　　Can make a calm, cold mirror their instructor;

For, when beloved, we deify what's human—
   When piqued, we mock like devils ! But I pluck'd a
Digression here. It's no use, my contending—
Fancy will ramble while the pen is mending !

LXXXI.

A small room on the left, (I'll get on faster
   If you're impatient,) very softly lit
By lamps conceal'd in bells of alabaster,
   Lipp'd like a lily, and " as white as it,"
With a sweet statue by a famous master,
   Just in the centre (but not dress'd a bit !)
This dim room drew aside our early comer,
Who thought it like a moonlight night in summer.

LXXXII.

And so it was. For, through an opening door,
   Came the soft breath of a conservatory,
And, bending its tall stem the threshold o'er,
   Swung in a crimson flower, the tropics' glory ;
And, as you gazed, the vista lengthen'd more,
   And statues, lamps, and flowers—but, to my story !
The room was cushion'd like a Bey's divan ;
And in it—(Heaven preserve us !)—sat a man !

LXXXIII.

At least, as far as boots and pantaloons
   Are symptoms of a man, there seem'd one there—
Whatever was the number of his Junes.
   She look'd again, and started ! In a chair,

Sleeping as if his eyelids had been moons,
    Reclined, with flakes of sunshine in his hair,
(Or, what look'd like it,) a fair youth, quite real,
But of a beauty like the Greek ideal.

LXXXIV.

He slept, like Love by slumber overtaken,
    His bow unbent, his quiver thrown aside;
The lip might to a manlier arch awaken—
    The nostril, so serene, dilate with pride:
But now he lay, of all his masks forsaken,
    And childhood's sleep was there, and naught beside;
And his bright lips lay smilingly apart,
Like a torn crimson leaf with pearly heart.

LXXXV.

Now Jules Beaulevres, Esq.—(this was he)—
    Had never been " put up " to London hours;
And thinking he was simply ask'd to tea,
    Had been, since seven, looking at the flowers—
No doubt extremely pleasant,—but, you see,
    A great deal of it rather overpowers;
And possibly, that very fine exotic
He sat just under, was a slight narcotic.

LXXXVI.

At any rate, when it was all admired,—
    As quite his notion of a heaven polite,
(*Minus* the angels,) he felt very tired—
    As one, who'd been all day sight-seeing *might !*

And having by the Countess been desired
　To make himself at home, he did so, quite.
He begg'd his early coming might not fetter her,
And she went out to dine, the old—*etcetera.*

LXXXVII.

And thinking of his mother—and his bill
　At Mivart's—and of all the sights amazing
Of which, the last few days, he had his fill—
　And choking when he thought of fame—and gazing
Upon his varnish'd boots, (as young men will,)
　And wond'ring how the shops could pay for glazing,
And also (here his thoughts were getting dim,)
Whether a certain smile was meant for him—

LXXXVIII.

And murm'ring over, with a drowsy bow,
　The speech he made the Countess, when he met her,
And smiling, with closed eyelids, (thinking how
　He should describe her in the morrow's letter)—
And sighing "Good-night!" (he was dreaming now)
　Jules dropp'd into a world he liked much better;
But left his earthly mansion unprotected:
Well, sir! 'twas robb'd—as might have been expected!

LXXXIX.

The Lady Jane gazed on the fair boy sleeping,
　And in his lips' rare beauty read his name;
And to his side with breathless wonder creeping,
　Resistless to her heart the feeling came,

That, to her yearning love's devoted keeping,
   Was given the gem within that fragile frame;
And bending, with almost a mother's bliss,
To his bright lips, she seal'd it with a kiss!

XC.

Oh, in that kiss how much of heaven united!
   What haste to pity—eagerness to bless!
What thirsting of a heart, long pent and slighted,
   For something fair, yet human, to caress!
How fathomless the love so briefly plighted!
   What kiss thrill'd ever more—sinn'd ever less!
So love the angels, sent with holy mercies!
And so love poets—in their early verses!

XCI.

If, in well-bred society, ("Hear! hear!")
   If, in this "wrong and pleasant" world of ours,
There beats a pulse that seraphs may revere—
   If Eden's birds, when frighted from its flowers,
Clung to one deathless seed, still blooming here—
   If Time cut ever down, 'mid blighted hours,
A bliss that will spring up in bliss again—
'Tis woman's love. This I believe. Amen.

XCII.

To guard from ill, to help, watch over, warn—
   To learn, for his sake, sadness, patience, pain—
To seek him with most love when most forlorn—
   Promised the mute kiss of the Lady Jane.

And thus, in sinless purity is born,
  Alway, the love of woman. So, again,
I say, that up to kissing—later even—
A woman's love may have its feet in heaven.

XCIII.

Jules open'd (at the kiss) his large blue eyes,
  And calmly gazed upon the face above him,
But never stirr'd, and utter'd no surprise—
  Although his situation well might move him.
He seem'd so cool, (my *lyre* shall tell no *lies*,)
  That Lady Jane half thought she shouldn't love him ;
When suddenly the Countess Pasibleu
Enter'd the room with " Dear me ! how d'ye do ? "

XCIV.

Up sprang the boy—amazement on his brow !
  But the next instant, through his lips there crept
A just awakening smile, and, with a bow,
  Calmly he said : " 'Twas only while I slept
The angels did not vanish—until now."
  A speech, I think, quite worthy an adept.
The Countess stared, and Lady Jane began
To fear that she had kiss'd a nice young man.

XCV.

Jules had that precious quality call'd *tact ;*
  And having made a very warm beginning,
He suddenly grew grave, and rather back'd ;
  As if incapable of further sinning.
'Twas well he did so, for, it is a fact,
  The ladies like, themselves, to do the winning.

In *female* Shakspeares, Desdemonas shine ;
And the Othellos " seriously incline."

XCVI.

So, with a manner quite reserved and plain,
　　Jules ask'd to be presented, and then made
Many apologies to Lady Jane
　　For the eccentric part that he had play'd.
Regretted he had slept—confess'd with pain
　　He took her for an angel—was afraid
He had been rude—abrupt—did he alarm
Her much ?—and might he offer her his arm ?

XCVII.

And as they ranged that sweet conservatory,
　　He heeded not the flowers he walk'd among :
But such an air of earnest listening wore he,
　　That a dumb statue must have found a tongue ;
And like a child that hears a fairy story,
　　His parted lips upon her utterance hung.
He seem'd to know by instinct, (else how was it ?)
That people love the bank where they deposit.

XCVIII.

And closer, as the moments faster wore,
　　The slender arm within her own she press'd ;
And yielding to the magic spell he bore—
　　The earnest truth upon his lips impress'd—
She lavishly *told* out the golden ore
　　Hoarded a lifetime in her guarded breast.
And Jules, throughout, was beautifully tender—
Although he did not always comprehend her.

XCIX.

And this in him was no deep calculation,
    But in good truth, as well as graceful seeming,
Abandonment complete to admiration—
    His soul gone from him as it goes in dreaming.
I wish'd to make this little explanation,
    Misgiving that his tact might go for scheming ;
I can assure you it was never plann'd ;
I have it from his angel (second hand).

C.

And from the same authentic source I know,
    That Lady Jane still thought him but a lad ;
Though why the deuce she didn't treat him so,
    Is quite enough to drive conjecture mad !
Perhaps she thought that it would make him grow
    To take more beard for granted than he had.
A funny friend to lend a nice young man to !
I'm glad I've got him safely through *one* Canto.

CANTO II.

I.

THE Countess Pasibleu's gay rooms were full,
    Not crowded.   It was neither rout nor ball—
Only " her Friday night."   The air was cool ;
    And there were people in the house of all
Varieties, except the pure John Bull.
    The number of young ladies, too, was small—
You seldom find *old* John, or his *young* daughters
Swimming in very literary waters.

II.

Indeed, with rare exceptions, women given
    To the society of famous men,
Are those who will confess to twenty-seven ;
    But add to this the next reluctant ten,
And still they're fit to make a poet's heaven,
    For sumptuously beautiful is then
The woman of proud mien and thoughtful brow ;
And one (still bright in her meridian now)

III.

Bent upon Jules, that night, her lustrous eye.
    A creature of a loftier mould was she
Than in his dreams had ever glided by ;
    And through his veins the blood flew startlingly,
And he felt sick at heart—he knew not why—
    For 'tis the sadness of the lost to see
Angels look on us with a cold regard,
(Not knowing those who never left their card.)

IV.

She had a low, sweet brow, with fringèd lakes
    Of an unfathom'd darkness couch'd below ;
And parted on that brow in jetty flakes
    The raven hair swept back with wavy flow,
Rounding a head of such a shape as makes
    The old Greek marble with the goddess glow.
Her nostril's breathing arch might threaten storm—
But love lay in her lips, all hush'd and warm.

V.

And small teeth, glittering white, and cheek whose red
    Seem'd Passion, there asleep, in rosy nest :

And neck set on as if to bear a head—
　May be a lily, may be Juno's crest,—
So slightly sprang it from its snow-white bed !
　So proudly rode above the swelling breast !
And motion, effortless as stars awaking
And melting out, at eve, and morning's breaking

VI.

And voice delicious quite, and smile that came
　Slow to the lips, as 'twere the heart smiled thro' :—
These charms I've been particular to name,
　For they are, like an inventory, true,
And of themselves were stuff enough for fame ;
　But she, so wondrous fair, has genius too,
And brilliantly her thread of life is spun—
In verse and beauty both, the " Undying One ! "

VII.

And song—for in those kindling lips there lay
　Music to wing all utterance outward breaking,
As if upon the ivory teeth did play
　Angels, who caught the words at their awaking,
And sped them with sweet melodies away—
　The hearts of those who listen'd with them taking.
Of proof to this last fact there's little lack ;
And Jules, poor lad ! ne'er got *his* truant back !

VIII.

That heart stays with her still.　'Tis one of two,
　(I should premise)—all poets being double,
Living in two worlds as of course they do,
　Fancy and fact, and rarely taking trouble
T' explain *in which* they're living, as to *you !*
　And this it is makes all the hubble-bubble,

For who can fairly write a bard's biography,
When, of his *fancy*-world, there's no geography ?

IX.

Jules was at perfect liberty *in fact*
   To love again, and still be true *in fancy ;*
Else were this story at its closing act,
   Nay, he *in fact* might wed, and *in romance* he
Might find the qualities his *sposa* lack'd—
   (A truth that I could easier make a man see,)
And woman's great mistake, if I may tell it, is
The calling such stray fancies "infidelities."

X.

Byron was man and bard, and Lady B.,
   In wishing to monopolise him wholly,
Committed bigamy, you plainly see.
   She, being *very* single, Guiccioli
Took off the odd one of the wedded three—
   A change, 'twould seem, quite natural and holy.
The *after* sin, which still his fame environs,
Was giving Guiccioli *both* the Byrons.

XI.

The stern wife drove him from her.　Had she loved
   With all the woman's tenderness the while,
He had not been the wanderer he proved.
   Like bird to sunshine fled he to a smile ;
And, lightly though the changeful fancy roved,
   The heart speeds home with far more light a wile.
The world well tried—the sweetest thing in life
Is the unclouded welcome of a wife.

XII.

To poets more than all—for truthful love
   Has, to their finer sense, a deeper sweetness;
Yet she who has the venturous wish to prove
   The poet's love when nearest to completeness,
Must wed the *man* and let the *fancy* rove—
   Loose to the air that wing of eager fleetness,
And smile it home when wearied out—with air,
But if you scold him, Madam! have a care!

XIII.

All this time the "Undying One" was singing.
   She ceased, and Jules felt every sound a pain
While that sweet cadence in his ear was ringing;
   So gliding from the arm of Lady Jane,
Which rather seem'd to have the whim of clinging,
   He made himself a literary lane—
Punching and shoving every kind of writer
Till he got out. (He might have been politer.)

XIV.

Free of "the press," he wander'd through the rooms,
   Longing for solitude, but studying faces;
And, smitten with the ugliness of Brougham's,
   He mused upon the cross with monkey races—
(Hieroglyphick'd on th' Egyptian tombs
   And shown in France with very striking traces.)
"Rejected" Smith's he thought a head quite glorious;
And Hook, all button'd up, he took for "Boreas."

XV.

He noted Lady Stepney's pretty hand,
   And Barry Cornwall's sweet and serious eye;

K

And saw Moore get down from his chair to stand,
   While a most royal duke went bowing by—
Saw Savage Landor, wanting soap and sand—
   Saw Lady Chatterton take snuff and sigh—
Saw graceful Bulwer say " Good-night," and vanish—
Heard Crofton Croker's brogue, and thought it Spanish.

XVI.

He saw Smith whispering something very queer,
   And Hayward creep behind to overhear him ;
Saw Lockhart whistling in a lady's ear,
   (Jules thought so, till, on getting very near him,
The error—not the mouth—became quite clear ;)
   He saw "*the* Duke" and had a mind to cheer him,
And fine Jane Porter with her cross and feather,
And clever Babbage, with his face of leather.

XVII.

And there was plump and saucy Mrs. Gore,
   And calm, old, lily-white Joanna Baillie,
And frisky Bowring, London's wisest bore ;
   And there was " devilish handsome " D'Israeli ;
And not a lion of all these did roar ;
   But laughing, flirting, gossiping so gaily,—
Poor Jules began to think 'twas only mockery
To talk of " porcelain "—'twas a world of crockery.

XVIII.

'*Tis* half a pity authors should be seen !
   Jules thought so, and I think so, too, with Jules.
They'd better do the immortal with a screen,
   And show but mortal in a world of fools ;

Men talk of "taste" for thunder—but they mean
　　Old Vulcan's apron and his dirty tools ;
They flock all wonder to the Delphic shade,
To know—just how the oracle is made !

XIX.

What we should think of Bulwer's works—without him,
　　His wife, his coat, his curls or other handle ;
What of our Cooper, knowing naught about him,
　　Save his enchanted quill and pilgrim's sandal ;
What of old Lardner, (gracious ! how they flout him !)
　　Without this broad—(and *Heavy-*) *side* of scandal ;
What of Will Shakspeare had he kept a " Boz"
Like Johnson—would be curious questions, coz !

XX.

Jove is, no doubt, a gainer by his cloud,
　　(Which ta'en away, might cause irreverent laughter,)
But, out of sight, he thunders ne'er so loud,
　　And no one asks the god to dinner after ;
And " Fame's proud temple," build it ne'er so proud,
　　Finds notoriety a useful rafter.
And when you've been abused awhile, you learn,
All blasts blow fair for you—*that blow astern !*

XXI.

No "*pro*" without its "*con ;*"—the *pro* is fame,
　　Pure, cold, unslander'd, like a virgin's frill ;
The *con* is beef and mutton, sometimes game,
　　Madeira, sherry, claret, what you will ;
The ladies' (albums) striving for your name ;
　　All, (save the woodcock,) yours without a bill ;

And "in the gate," an unbelieving Jew,
Your "Mordecai!"—Why, clearly *con's* your cue!

XXII.

I've "reason'd" myself neatly "round the ring,"
  While Jules came round to Lady Jane once more,
And supper being but a heavy thing,
  (To lookers-on,) I'll show him to the door,
And his first night to a conclusion bring;
  Not (with your kind permission, sir) before
I tell you what her Ladyship said to him
  As home to Brook Street her swift horses drew him.

XXIII.

"You're comfortably lodged, I trust," she said:
  "And Mrs. Mivart—is she like a mother?
Have you mosquito curtains to your bed?
  Do you sleep well without your little brother?
What do you eat for breakfast—baker's bread?
  I'll send you some home-made, if you would rather.
What do you do to-morrow?—say at five,
Or four—say four—I call for you to drive!

XXIV.

"There's the New Garden, and the Coliseum—
  Perhaps you don't care much for Panoramas?
But there's an armadillo—you *must* see him!
  And those big-eyed giraffes and heavenly lamas!
And—are you fond of music?—the *Te Deum*
  Is beautifully play'd by Lascaramhas,
At the new Spanish chapel. This damp air!
And you've no hat on!—let me feel your hair!

XXV.

" Poor boy ! "—but Jules's head was on her breast,
  Rock'd like a nautilus in calm mid-ocean ;
And while its curls within her hands she press'd,
  The Lady Jane experienced some emotion :
For, did he sleep ? or wish to be caress'd ?
  What meant the child ?—she'd not the slightest notion !
Arrived at home, he rose, without a shake—
Trembling and slightly flush'd—but wide awake.

XXVI.

Loose rein ! put spur ! and follow, gentle reader !
  For I must take a flying leap in rhyme ;
And be to you both Jupiter and *leader*,
  Annihilating space, (we all kill time,)
And overtaking Jules in Rome, where he'd a
  Delight or two, besides the pleasant clime.
The Lady Jane and he (I scorn your cavils—
The Earl was with them, sir !) were on their travels.

XXVII.

You know, perhaps, the winds are no narcotic,
  As swallow'd 'twixt the Thames and Firth of Forth ;
And Jules had proved a rather frail exotic—
  Too delicate to winter so far north ;
The Earl was breaking, and half idiotic,
  And Lady Jane's condition little worth ;
So, through celestial Paris, (speaking victual-ly,)
They sought the sunnier clime of ill-fed Italy.

XXVIII.

O Italy !—but no !—I'll tell its faults—
  It has them, though the blood so " nimbly capers "

Beneath those morning heavens and starry vaults,
   That we forget big rooms and little tapers;
Forget how drowsily the Romans waltz;
   Forget they've neither shops nor morning papers;
Forget how dully sits, 'mid ancient glory,
This rich man's heaven—this poor man's purgatory!

XXIX.

Fashion the world as one bad man would have it, he
   Would silence Harry's tongue, and Tom's, and Dick's;
And doubtless it is pleasing to depravity
   To know a land where people are but sticks—
Where you've no need of fair words, flattery, suavity,
   But spend your money, if you like, with kicks—
Where they pass by their own proud, poor nobility,
To welcome golden "Snooks" with base servility.

XXX.

Jules was not in the poor man's category—
   So Rome's condition never spoilt his supper.
The deuce (for him) might take the Curtian glory
   Of riding with a nation on his crupper.
He lived upon a Marquis's first storey—
   The venerable Marquis in the upper—
And found it pass'd the time, (and so would you,)
To do some things at Rome that Romans do.

XXXI.

The Marquis upon whom he chanced to quarter,
   (He took his lodgings separate from the Earl,)
The Marquis had a friend, who had a daughter—
   The friend a noble like himself, the girl

A diamond of the very purest water ;
  (Or purest milk, if you prefer a pearl ;)
And these two friends, tho' poor, were hand and glove,
And of a pride their fortunes much above.

XXXII.

The Marquis had not much besides his palace,
  The Count, beyond his daughter, simply naught ;
And, one day, died this very Count Pascalis,
  Leaving his friend his daughter, as he ought ;
And, though the Fates had done the thing in malice,
  The old man took her, without second thought,
And married her. " She's freer thus," he said,
" And will be young to marry when I'm dead."

XXXIII.

Meantime, she had a title, house, and carriage,
  And far from wearing chains, had newly burst 'em—
For, as of course you know, before their marriage
  Girls are sad prisoners by Italian custom—
Not meaning their discretion to disparage,
  But just because they're sure they couldn't trust 'em.
When wedded, they are free enough—moreover
The marriage contract specifies *one* lover.

XXXIV.

Not that the Marchioness had one—no, no !
  Nor wanted one. It is not my intention
To hint it in this tale. Jules lodged below—
  But his vicinity's not my invention ;
And, if it seems to you more *apropos*
  Than I have thought it worth my while to mention,
Why, *you* think as the world did—*verbum sat*—
But still it needn't be so—for all that,

XXXV.

'Most any female neighbour, up a stair,
   Occasions thought in him who lodges under;
And Jules, by accident, had walk'd in where
   (A "*flight* too high" 's a very common blunder.)
He saw a lady whom he thought as fair
   As "from her shell rose" Mrs. Smith of Thunder,
Though Venus, I would say were Vulcan by,
Was no more like the Marchioness than I.

XXXVI.

For this grave sin there needed much remission;
   And t' assure it, oft the offender went.
The Marquis had a very famous Titian,
   And Jules so often came to pay his rent,
The old man recommended a physician,
   Thinking his intellect a little bent;
And, pitying, he thought and talk'd about him,
Till, finally, he couldn't live without him.

XXXVII.

And, much to the neglect of Lady Jane,
   Jules paid him back his love; and there, all day,
The fair young Marchioness, with fickle brain,
   Tried him with changeful mood, now coy, now gay:
And the old man lived o'er his youth again,
   Seeing those grown-up children at their play,
His wife sixteen, Jules looking scarcely more,
'Twas frolic infancy to eighty-four.

XXXVIII.

There seems less mystery in matrimony,
   With people living nearer the equator;

And early, like the most familiar crony,
  Unheralded by butler, groom, or waiter,
Jules join'd the Marquis at his macaroni,—
  The Marchioness at toast and coffee later;
And if his heart throbb'd wild sometimes, he hid it;
And if her dress required "doing"—did it.

XXXIX.

Now, though the Marchioness in church *did* faint once,
  And, as Jules bore her out, they didn't group ill;
And though the spouses (as a pair) were quaint ones—
  She scarce a woman, and his age octuple—
'Twas odd, extremely odd, of their acquaintance,
  To call Jules *lover* with so little scruple!
He'd a caressing way—but la! you know it's
A sort of manner natural to poets!

XL.

God made them prodigal in their bestowing:
  And, if their smiles were riches, few were poor!
They turn to all the sunshine that is going—
  Swoop merrily at all that shows a lure—
Their love at heart and lips is overflowing—
  Their motto, "Trust the *future*—*now* is sure!"
Their natural pulse is high intoxication
(Sober'd by debt and mortal botheration).

XLI.

Of such men's pain and pleasure, hope and passion,
  The symptoms are not read by "those who run;"
And 'tis a pity it were not the fashion
  To count them but as children of the sun—
Not to be baited like the "bulls of Bashan,"
  Nor liable, like clods, for "one pound one"—

But reverenced—as Indians rev'rence fools—
Inspired, tho' God knows how.   Well—such was Jules.

XLII.

The Marquis thought him sunshine at the window—
 The window of his heart—and let him in !
The Marchioness loved sunshine like a Hindoo,
 And she thought loving him could be no sin ;
And as she loved not yet as those who sin do,
 'Twas very well—was't not ?   Stick there a pin !
It strikes me that so far—to this last stanza—
The hero seems a well-disposed young man, sir !

XLIII.

I have not bored you much with his " abilities,"
 Though I set out to treat you to a poet,
The first course commonly is " puerilities "—
 (A soup well pepper'd—all the critics know it !)
Brought in quite hot.   (The simple way to chill it is,
 For " spoons " to stir, and *puffy* lips to blow it.)
Then, poet stuff'd, and by his kidney roasted,
And last (with " *lagrima*,") " the devil " toasted

XLIV.

High-scream between the devil and the roast,
 But no *Sham-pain !*——Hold there ! the fit is o'er.
Obsta principiis—one pun breeds a host—
 (Alarmingly prolific for a bore !)
But he who never sins can little boast
 Compared to him who goes and sins no more !
The " sinful Mary " walks more white in heaven
Than some who never " sinn'd and were forgiven ! "

XLV.

Jules had objections very strong to playing
   His character of poet—therefore I
Have rather dropp'd that thread, as I was saying.
   But though he'd neither frenzy in his eye,
Nor much of outer mark the bard betraying—
   (A thing he piqued himself on, by the by—)
His conversation frequently arose
To what was thought a goodly flight for prose.

XLVI.

His *beau ideal* was to sink the attic—
   (Though not by birth, nor taste, " the *salt* above "—)
To pitilessly cut the air erratic
   Which ladies, fond of authors, so much love,
And be, in style, calm, cold, aristocratic—
   Serene in faultless boots and primrose glove.
But th' exclusive's made of starch, not honey!
And Jules was cordial, joyous, frank, and funny.

XLVII.

This was one secret of his popularity,
   Men hate a manner colder than their own,
And ladies—bless their hearts! love chaste hilarity
   Better than sentiment—if truth were known!
And Jules had one more slight peculiarity—
   He'd little "approbativeness"—or none—
And what the critics said concern'd him little—
Provided it touch'd not his drink and victual.

XLVIII.

Critics, I say—of course he was in print—
   " Poems," of course—of course " anonymous "—

Of course he found a publisher by dint
　Of search most diligent, and far more fuss
Than chemists make in melting you a flint.
　Since that experiment he reckons *plus*
Better manure than *minus* for his bays—
In short, seeks immortality—"that pays."

XLIX.

He writes in prose—the public like it better.
　Well—*let* the public!　You may take a poet,
And he shall write his grandmother a letter,
　And, if he's anything *but* rhyme—he'll show it.
Prose may be poetry without its fetter,
　And be it pun or pathos, high or low wit,
The thread will show its gold, however twisted—
(I wish the public flatter'd me that this did!)

L.

No doubt there's pleasant stuff that ill unravels.
　I fancy most of Moore's would read so-so,
Done into prose of pious Mr. Flavel's—
　(That is my Sunday reading—so I know,)
Yet there's Childe Harold—excellent good travels—
　And what could spoil sweet Robinson Crusoe?
But though a clever *verse-r* makes a *prose-r*,
About the *vice-versa*, I don't know, sir!

LI.

Verser's a better word than *versifier*,
　(Unless 'tis *verse on fire*, you mean to say,)
And I've long thought there's something to desire
　In poet's nomenclature, by the way.
It sounds but queer to laud "*the well-known lyre*"—
　Call a dog "poet!" he will run away—

And "songster," "rhymester," "bard," and "poetaster,"
Are customers they're shy of at the Astor.

LII.

A "scribbler's" is a skittish reputation,
　And weighs a man down like a hod of mortar.
Commend a suitor's wit, imagination—
　The merchant may think of him for his daughter;
But say that "he writes poetry"— ——n!
　Her "Pa" would rather throw her in the water!
And yet when poets wed, as facts will prove,
Their bills stand all *at* pa, *they* much *above!*

LIII.

Jules had a hundred minds to cut the muses;
　And sometimes did, "for ever!"—(for a week!)
He found for time so many other uses.
　His superfluity was his *physique;*
And exercise, if violent, induces
　Blood to the head and flush upon the cheek;
And, (though details are neither here nor there,)
Makes a man sit uneasy on his chair;

LIV.

Particularly that of breaking horses.
　The rate of circulation in the blood,
Best suited to the meditative forces,
　Is quite as far from mercury as mud—
That of the starry, not the racing-courses.
　No man can trim his style 'mid fire and flood,
Nor in a passion, nor just after marriage;
And, as to Cæsar's writing in his carriage,

LV.

Credat Judæus! Thought is free and easy;
  But language, unless wrought with *labor limæ*,
Is not the kind of thing, sir, that would please ye!
  The bee makes honey, but his toil is *thymy*,
And nothing is well done until it tease ye;
  (Tho' if there's one who would 'twere not so, I'm he!)
Now Jules, I say, found out that filly-breaking,
Though monstrous fun, was not a poet's making.

LVI.

True—some *drink* up to composition's glow;
  Some *talk* up to it—*wide* Neckar's daughter!
But when the temp'rature's a fourth too low,
  Of course you make up the deficient quarter!
Like Byron's atmosphere, which, chemists know,
  Required hydrogen—(more gin and water.)
And Jules's sanguine humour was too high,
So, of the bottle he had need be shy!

LVII.

And of society, which makes him thin
  With fret and fever, and of sunny sky—
Father of idleness, the poet's sin!
  (John Bull should be industrious, by the by,
If clouds *without* concentrate thought *within.*)
  In short, the lad could fag—(I mean soar high)—
Only by habits, which (if Heaven let *her* choose)
His mother would bequeath as Christian virtues!

LVIII.

Now men have oft been liken'd unto streams:
  (And, truly, both are prone to run down hill,

And seldom brawl when dry, or so it seems !)
  And Jules, when he had brooded, long and still
At the dim fountain of the poet's dreams,
  Felt suddenly his veins with frenzy fill ;
And, urged, as by the torrent's headlong force,
Ruthlessly rode—if he could find a horse.

LIX.

Yes, sir—he had his freshets like a river,
  And horses were his passion—so he rode,
When he his prison'd spirits would deliver,
  As if he fled from—some man whom he owed—
And glorious, to him, the bounding quiver
  Of the young steed in terror first bestrode !
Thrilling as inspiration the delay—
The arrowy spring—the fiery flight away !

LX.

Such riding galls the Muses, (though we know
  Old Pegasus's build is short and stocky,)
But I'd a mind by these details to show
  What Jules might turn out, were the Muses baulky.
This hint to his biographer I throw—
  In Jules, the bard, was spoil'd a famous. jockey !
Though not at all to imitate Apollo !
Horse him as well, he'd beat *that* dabster hollow !

LXI.

'Tis one of the proprieties of story
  To mark the change in heroes, stage by stage ;
And therefore I have tried to lay before ye
  The qualities of Jules's second age.
It *should* wind up with some *memento mori*—
  But we'll defer that till we draw the sage.

The moral's the last thing, (I say with pain,)
And now let's turn awhile to Lady Jane.

LXII.

The Earl, I've said, was in his idiocy,
　　And Lady Jane not well.　They therefore hired
The summer palace of Rospigliosi,
　　To get the sun as well as be retired.
You shouldn't fail, I think, this spot to go see—
　　That's if you care to have your fancy fired—
It's out of Rome—it strikes me on a steep hill—
A sort of place to go with nice people.

LXIII.

It looks affectionate, with all its splendour—
　　As lovable as ever look'd a nest;
A palace, I protest, that makes you tender,
　　And long for——fol de rol, and all the rest.
Guido's Aurora's there—you couldn't mend her:
　　And Samson, by Caracci—not his best;
But pictures I can talk of to the million—
To *you*, I'll just describe one small pavilion.

LXIV.

It's in the garden just below the palace;
　　I think, upon the second terrace—no—
The first—yes, 'tis the first—the orange alleys
　　Lead from the first flight down—precisely so!
Well—half-way is a fountain, where, with malice
　　In all his looks, a Cupid—'hem! you know
You needn't notice that—you hurry by,
And lo! a fairy structure fills your eye.

LXV.

A crescent colonnade folds in the sun,
  To keep it for the wooing South wind only—
A thing I wonder is not oftener done,
  (The crescent, not the wooing—that's *my own* lie,)
For there are months, and January's one,
  When winds are chill, and life indoors gets lonely,
And one quite longs, if wind would keep away,
To sing i' the sunshine, like old King René.

LXVI.

The columns are of marble, white as light :
  The structure low, yet airy, and the floor
A tesselated pavement, curious quite,—
  Of the same fashion in and out of door.
The Lady Jane, who kept not warm by sight,
  Had carpeted this pavement snugly o'er,
And introduced a stove, (an open Rumford)—
So the pavilion had an air of comfort.

LXVII.

"The frescoes on the ceiling really breathe,"
  The guide-books say.   Of course they really *see :*
And, as I tell you what went on beneath,
  Of course those naked goddesses told *me.*
They saw two rows of dazzling English teeth,
  Employ'd, each morn, on "English toast and tea ; "
And once, when Jules came in, they strain'd their eyes,
But didn't see the teeth, to their surprise.

LXVIII.

The Lady Jane smiled not.   Her lashes hung
  Low to the soft eye, and so still they lay,

L

Jules knew a tear was hid their threads among,
  And that she fear'd 'twould gush and steal away.
The kindly greeting trembled on her tongue,
  The hand's faint pressure chill'd his touch like clay,
And Jules with wonder felt the world all changing,
With but the cloud of one fond heart's estranging.

LXIX.

Oh it is darkness to lose love!—howe'er
  We little prize the fond heart—fond no more!
The bird, dark-wing'd on earth, looks white in air!
  Unrecognized are angels, till they soar!
And few so rich they may not well beware
  Of lightly losing the heart's golden ore!
Yet—hast thou love too poor for thy possessing?—
Loose it, like friends to death, with kiss and blessing!

LXX.

You're naturally surprised, that Lady Jane
  Loved Mr. Jules.   (He's *Mr.* now—not *Master !*)
The fact's abruptly introduced, it's plain;
  And possibly I should have made it last a
Whole Canto, more or less—but I'll explain.
  Lumping the sentiment one gets on faster!
Though it's in narrative an art quite subtle,
To work all even, like a weaver's shuttle.

LXXI.

Good "characters" in tales are "well brought up"—
  (Though, by this rule, my Countess Pasibleu
Is a bad character—yet, just to sup,
  I much prefer her house to a church pew—)
But, pouring verse for readers, cup by cup,—
  So much a week,—what is a man to do?

" 'Tis wish'd that if a story you begin, you'd
Make separate scenes of each 'To be continued.' "

LXXII.

So writes plain " Jonathan," who tills my brains
  With view to crop—(the seed being ready money—)
And if the " small-lot system " bring him gains,
  He has a right to fence off grave from funny—
Working me up, as 'twere, in window-panes,
  And, I must own, where one has room to run, he
Is apt, as Cooper does, to spread it thin,
So now I'll go to *lumping* it again !

LXXIII.

" Love grows, by what " it gives to feed another,
  And not by what " it feeds on."   'Tis divine,
If anything's divine besides the mother
  Whose breast, self-blessing, is its holy sign.
Much better than a sister loves a brother
  The Lady Jane loved Jules, and " line by line,
Precept by precept," furnish'd him advice ;
Also much other stuff he thought more nice.

LXXIV.

She got him into sundry pleasant clubs,
  By pains that women *can* take, though but few will !
She made most of him when he got most rubs ;
  And once, in an inevitable duel,
She follow'd him alone to Wormwood Scrubs—
  But not to hinder !   Faith ! she was a jewel !
I wish the star all manner of festivity
That shone upon her Ladyship's nativity !

LXXV.

All sorts of enviable invitations,
    Tickets, and privileges, got she him;
Gave him much satin waistcoat, work'd with patience,
    (Becoming to a youth so jimp and slim)—
Cut for his sake some prejudiced relations,
    And found for him in church the psalm and hymn;
Sent to his "den" some things not found in Daniel's,
And kept him in kid gloves, cologne, and flannels.

LXXVI.

To set him down upon her way *chez elle,*
    She stay'd unreasonably late at parties;
To introduce him to a waltzing belle
    She sometimes made a *cessio dignitatis;*
And one kind office more that I must tell—
    She sent her maid, (and very stern your heart is
If charity like this you find a sin in,)
In church-time, privately, to air his linen.

LXXVII.

Was Jules ungrateful? No! Was he obtuse?
    Did he believe that women's hearts were flowing
With tenderness, like water in a sluice,—
    Like the sun's shining,—like the breeze's blowing,—
And fancy thanking them was not much use?
    Had he the luck of intimately knowing
Another woman, quite as kind, and nicer?
Had he a "friend" *sub rosa?* No, sir! Fie, sir!

LXXVIII.

Then why neglect her? Having said he did,
    I will explain, as Brutus did his stab,—

(Though by my neighbours I'm already chid
   For getting on so very like a crab)—
Jules didn't call, as oft as he was bid,
   Because in Rome he didn't keep a cab—
A fact that quite explains why friendships, marriages,
And other ties depend on keeping carriages.

LXXIX.

Without a carriage men should have no card,
   Nor " owe a call " at all—except for love.
And friends who need that you the " lean earth lard "
   To give their memories a pasteboard shove,
On gentlemen a-foot bear rather hard !
   It's paying high for Broadway balls, by Jove !
To walk next day half way to Massachusett
And leave your name—on ladies that won't use it.

LXXX.

It really should be taught in infant schools
   That the majority means men, not dollars ;
And, therefore, that, to let the rich make rules,
   Is silly in " poor pretty little scholars."
And this you see is *apropos* of Jules,
   Who call'd as frequently as richer callers
While he'd a cab ;—but courtesy's half horse—
A secret those who ride keep snug, of course.

LXXXI.

I say while he was Centaur, (horse and man,)
   Jules never did neglect the Lady Jane ;
And, at the start it was my settled plan,
   (Though I've lost sight of it, I see with pain,)
To show how moderate attentions can,
   If once she love, a woman's heart retain.

True love is weak and humble, though so brittle ;
And asks, 'tis wonderful how very little !

LXXXII.

For instance—Jules's every-day routine
  Was, breakfast at his lodgings, rather early ;
A short walk in the nearest Park, the Green ;
  (Where, if address'd he was extremely surly ;)
Five minutes at the Club, perhaps fifteen ;
  Then giving his fine silk moustache a curl, he
Stepp'd in his cab and drove to Belgrave Square,
Where he walk'd in with quite a household air.

LXXXIII.

And here he pass'd an hour—or two, or three—
  Just as it served his purpose, or his whim ;
And sweeter haunt on earth could scarcely be
  Than that still boudoir, rose-lit, scented, dim—
Its mistress, elsewhere all simplicity,
  Dress'd ever sumptuously *there*—for him !
With all that taste could mould, or gold could buy,
Pampering fondly his reluctant eye.

LXXXIV.

And on the silken cushions at her feet
  He daily dream'd these morning hours away,
Troubling himself but little to be sweet.
  Poets are fond of reverie, they say,
But not with ladies whom they *rarely* meet.
  And if you love one, madam, (as you may !)
And wish his wings to pin as with a skewer,
  Be careful of all manner of *toujours !*

LXXXV.

" *Toujours perdrix*," snipe, woodcock, trout, or rabbit
  Offends the simplest palate, it appears,
And, (if a secret, I'm disposed to blab it,)
  It's much the same with smiles, sighs, quarrels, tears.
The fancy mortally abhors a *habit !*
  (Not that which Seraphina's bust inspheres !)
E'en one-tuned music-boxes breed satiety,
Unless you keep of them a great variety.

LXXXVI.

Daily to Jules the sun rose in the East,
  And brought new milk and morning paper daily ;
The "yield " of both the Editor and beast,
  Great mysteries, unsolved by Brown or Paley ;
But Jules—not plagued about it in the least—
  Read his gazette, and drank his tea quite gaily ;
And Lady Jane's fond love and cloudless brow
Grew to be like the Editor and cow.

LXXXVII.

I see you understand it. One may dash on
  A colour here—stroke there—and lo ! the story !
And, speaking morally, this outline fashion
  Befits a world so cramm'd yet transitory.
I've sketch'd for you a deep and tranquil passion
  Kindled while nursing up a bard for glory ;
And, having whisk'd you for that end to London,
Let's back to Italy, and see it undone.

LXXXVIII.

Fair were the frescoes of Rospigliosi—
  Bright the Italian sunshine on the wall—

The day delicious and the room quite cozy—
    And yet there were two bosoms full of gall !
So lurks the thorn in paths long soft and rosy !
    Jules was not one whom trifles could appal,
But few things will make creep the lion's mane
Like ladies in a miff who won't explain !

LXXXIX.

Now I have seen a hadji and a cadi—
    Have sojourn'd among strangers, oft and long—
Have known most sorts of women, fair and shady,
    And mingled in most kinds of mortal throng—
But, in my life, I never saw a lady
    Who had, *the least*, the air of being wrong !
The fact is, there's a nameless grace in evil
We never caught—'twas *she* who saw the devil !

XC.

In pedigree of sin we're mere beginners—
    For what was Adam to the " morning star " ?
She would take precedence—if sins were dinners,
    And hence that self-assured *" de haut en bas "*
So unattainable by men, as sinners.
    Of course, she plays the devil in a *fracas*—
Frowns better, looks more innocent, talks faster,
And argues like her grandmother's old master !

XCI.

And in proportion as the angel fades—
    As love departs—the crest of woman rises—
Even in passion's softer, lighter shades,
    With aristocracy's well-bred disguises ;
For, with no tragic fury, no tirades,
    A lady *looks* a man into a crisis !

And, to 'most any animal carnivorous
Before a belle aggrieved, the Lord deliver us !

XCII.

Jules had one thing particular to say,
  The morn I speak of, but, in fact, was there,
With twenty times the mind to be away.
  Uncomfortable seem'd the stuff'd arm-chair
In which the Earl would sometimes pass the day ;
  And there was something Roman in the air ;
For every effort to express his errand
Ended in " Um ! " as 'twere a Latin gerund.

XCIII.

He had received a little billet-doux
  The night before—as plain as A B C—
(I mean, it would appear as plain to you,
  Though very full of meaning, you'll agree)—
Informing him that by advice quite new
  The Earl was going now to try the sea ;
And begging him to have his passport vised
For Venice, by Bologna—if he pleased !

XCIV.

Smooth as a melody of Mother Goose's
  The gentle missive elegantly ran—
A sort of note the writer don't care who sees,
  For you may pick a flaw in't if you can—
But yet a stern *experimentum crucis*,
  Quite in the style of Metternich, or Van,—
And meant—without more flummery or fuss—
Stay with your Marchioness—or come with us !

XCV.

Here was to be "a parting such as wrings
    The blood from out young hearts "—for Jules *would* stay!
The bird she took unfledged had got its wings,
    And, though its cage be gold, it must away!
But this, and similar high-colour'd things,
    Refinement makes it difficult to say;
For, higher "high life" is, (this side an attic,)
The more it shrinks from all that looks dramatic.

XCVI.

Hence, words grow cold as agony grows hot,
    'Twixt those who see in ridicule a Hades;
And though the truth but coldly end the plot,
    (There really is no pathos for you, ladies!)
Jules cast the die with simple "I think not!"
    And her few words were guarded as he made his,
For rank has one cold law of Moloch's making—
Death, before outcry, while the heart is breaking!

XCVII.

She could not tell that boy how hot the tear
    That seem'd within her eyeball to have died—
She could not tell him her exalted sphere
    Had not a hope his boyish love beside:
The grave of anguish is a human ear—
    Hers lay unburied in a pall of pride!
And life, for her, thenceforth, was cold and lonely,
With her heart lock'd on that dumb sorrow only!

XCVIII.

Calm, in her "pride of place," moves Lady Jane—
    Paler, but beautifully pale, and cold—

So cold, the gazer believes joy nor pain
   Has o'er that pulse of marble ever roll'd.
She loved too late to dream of love again,
   And rich, fair, noble, and alone, grows old !
A star, on which a spirit had alighted
Once, in all time, were like a life so blighted !

XCIX.

So, from the poet's woof was broke a thread
   Which we have follow'd in its rosy weaving !
Yet merrily, still on, the shuttle sped.
   Jules was not made of stuff to die of grieving ;
But, that an angel from his path had fled,
   He was not long in mournfully believing.
And " angel watch and ward " had fled with her—
For, virtuously loved, 'tis hard to err !

C.

Poets are moths, (or so some poet sings,
   Or so some pleasant allegory goes,)
And Jules at many a bright light burnt his wings.
   His first chaste scorching the foregoing shows ;
But, while one passion best in metre rings,
   Another is best told in lucid prose.
As to the Marchioness, I've half a plan, sir !
To limn her in the quaint Spenserian stanza.

THE END.

TO THE READER.

And now, dear reader ! as a brick may be
   A sample of a house—a bit of glass
Of a broad mirror—it has seem'd to me
   These fragments for a tale may shift to pass.
(I am a poet much *cut up*, pardie !)
   But "shorts" is poor "to running loose to grass."
Where there's a meadow to range freely over,
You pick to please you—timothy or clover.

Without the slightest hint at transmigration,
   I wish hereafter we may meet *in calf!*
That you may read me with some variation—
   This when you're moody—*that* when you would laugh.
In that case, I may swell this true narration,
   And blow off here and there a speech of chaff.
I trust you think, that, were there more 'twere better, or
If *cetera desunt*, decent were the cetera !

P. S.—I really had forgotten quite
   To say to you, from Countess Pasibleu—
(Dying, 'tis thought, but quite too ill to write)—
   Her Ladyship's best compliments to you,
And she's *toujours chez elle* on Friday night,
   (Buckingham Crescent, May Fair, No. 2.)
This, (as her written missive would have said,)
Always in case her Ladyship's not dead.

LORD IVON AND HIS DAUGHTER.   P. 173.

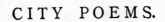

CITY POEMS.

CITY POEMS.

—►◄—

Argument.—The poet starts from the Bowling Green,* to take his sweet-heart up to Thompson's † for an ice, or (if she is inclined for more) ices. He confines his muse to matters which any every-day man and young woman may see in taking the same promenade for the same innocent refreshment.

COME out, love—the night is enchanting !
    The moon hangs just over Broadway ;
The stars are all lighted and panting—
    (Hot weather up there, I dare say !)
'Tis seldom that " coolness" entices,
    And love is no better for chilling—
But come up to Thompson's for ices,
    And cool your warm heart for a shilling !

What perfume comes balmily o'er us ?
    Mint juleps from City Hotel !
A loafer is smoking before us—
    (A nasty cigar, by the smell !)
O Woman ! thou secret past knowing !
    Like lilacs that grow by the wall,
You breathe every air that is going,
    Yet gather but sweetness from all !

On, on ! by St. Paul's, and the Astor !
    Religion seems very ill-plann'd !
For one day we list to the pastor,
    For six days we list to the band !

* At the time, 1830–40, surrounded by fashionable residences.
† A famous restaurant.

The sermon may dwell on the future,
  The organ your pulses may calm—
When—pest !—that remember'd cachucha
  Upsets both the sermon and psalm !

Oh, pity the love that must utter
  While goes a swift omnibus by !
(Though sweet is *I scream* * when the flutter
  Of fans shows thermometers high)—
But if what I bawl, or I mutter,
  Falls into your ear but to die,
Oh, the dew that falls into the gutter
  Is not more unhappy than I !

———

THE WHITE CHIP HAT.

I PASS'D her one day in a hurry,
  When late for the post with a letter—
I think near the corner of Murray—
  And up rose my heart as I met her !
I ne'er saw a parasol handled
  So like to a duchess's doing—
I ne'er saw a slighter foot sandall'd,
  Or so fit to exhale in the shoeing—
      Lovely thing !

Surprising !—one woman can dish us
  So many rare sweets up together !
Tournure absolutely delicious—
  Chip hat without flower or feather—
Well-gloved and enchantingly boddiced,
  Her waist like the cup of a lily—

* *Query.*—Should this be *Ice cream,* or *I scream ?*—*Printer's Devil.*

And an air, that, while daintily modest,
    Repell'd both the saucy and silly—
        Quite the thing !

For such a rare wonder you'll say, sir,
    There's reason in straining one's tether—
And, to see her again in Broadway, sir,
    Who would not be lavish of leather !
I met her again, and as *you* know
    I'm sage as old Voltaire at Ferney—
But I said a bad word—for my Juno
    Look'd sweet on a sneaking attorney—
        Horrid thing !

Away flies the dream I had nourish'd—
    My castles like mockery fall, sir !
And, now, the fine airs that she flourish'd
    Seem varnish and crockery all, sir !
The bright cup which angels might handle
    Turns earthy when finger'd by asses—
And the star that " swaps " light with a candle
    Thenceforth for a pennyworth passes !—
        Not the thing !

———

LADY IN THE WHITE DRESS, I HELPED INTO THE OMNIBUS.

I KNOW her not ! Her hand has been in mine,
And the warm pressure of her taper arm
Has thrill'd upon my fingers, and the hem
Of her white dress has lain upon my feet,
Till my hush'd pulse, by the caressing folds,

M

Was kindled to a fever! I, to her,
Am but the undistinguishable leaf
Blown by upon the breeze—yet I have sat,
And in the blue depths of her stainless eyes,
(Close as a lover in his hour of bliss,
And steadfastly as look the twin stars down
Into unfathomable wells,) have gazed!
And I have felt from out its gate of pearl
Her warm breath on my cheek, and while she sat
Dreaming away the moments, I have tried
To count the long dark lashes in the fringe
Of her bewildering eyes! The kerchief sweet
That enviably visits her red lip
Has slumbered, while she held it, on my knee,—
And her small foot has crept between mine own—
And yet, she knows me not!

                  Now, thanks to Heaven
For blessings chainless in the rich man's keeping—
Wealth that the miser cannot hide away!
Buy, if they will, the invaluable flower—
They cannot store its fragrance from the breeze!
Wear, if they will, the costliest gem of Ind—
It pours its light on every passing eye!
And he who on this beauty sets his name—
Who dreams, perhaps, that for his use alone
Such loveliness was first of angels born—
Tell him, oh whisperer at his dreaming ear,
That I, too, in her beauty, sun my eye,
And, unrebuked, may worship her in song—
Tell him that Heaven, along our darkling way,
Hath set bright lamps with loveliness alight—
And all may in their guiding beams rejoice;
But he—as 'twere a watcher by a lamp—
Guards but this bright one's shining.

TO THE LADY IN THE CHEMISETTE WITH BLACK BUTTONS.

I KNOW not who thou art, oh lovely one !
Thine eyes were droop'd, thy lips half sorrowful,
Yet thou didst eloquently smile on me
While handing up thy sixpence through the hole
Of that o'er-freighted omnibus ! Ah me !
The world is full of meetings such as this—
A thrill, a voiceless challenge and reply—
And sudden partings after ! We may pass,
And know not of each other's nearness now—
Thou in the Knickerbocker Line, and I,
Lone, in the Waverley ! Oh, life of pain !
And even should I pass where thou dost dwell—
Nay—see thee in the basement taking tea—
So cold is this inexorable world,
I must glide on ! I dare not feast mine eye !
I dare not make articulate my love,
Nor o'er the iron rails that hem thee in
Venture to fling to thee my innocent card—
Not knowing thy papa !

               Hast thou papa ?
Is thy progenitor alive, fair girl ?
And what doth he for lucre ? Lo again !
A shadow o'er the face of this fair dream !
For thou mayst be as beautiful as Love
Can make thee, and the ministering hands
Of millinors, incapable of more,
Be lifted at thy shapeliness and air,
And still 'twixt me and thee, invisibly,
May rise a wall of adamant. My breath
Upon my pale lip freezes as I name

Manhattan's orient verge, and eke the west
In its far down extremity.   Thy sire
May be the signer of a temperance pledge,
And clad all decently may walk the earth—
Nay—may be number'd with that blessed few
Who never ask for discount—yet, alas !
If, homeward wending from his daily cares,
He go by Murphy's Line, thence eastward tending—
Or westward from the Line of Kipp & Brown,—
My vision is departed !   Harshly falls
The doom upon the ear, " She's not genteel ! "
And pitiless is woman who doth keep
Of " good society " the golden key !
And gentlemen are bound, as are the stars,
To stoop not after rising !

                    But farewell,
And I shall look for thee in streets where dwell
The passengers by Broadway Lines alone !
And if my dreams be true, and thou, indeed,
Art only not more lovely than genteel—
Then, lady of the snow-white chemisette,
The heart which vent'rously cross'd o'er to thee
Upon that bridge of sixpence, may remain—
And, with up-town devotedness and truth,
My love shall hover round thee !

———

YOU KNOW IF IT WAS YOU.

As the chill'd robin, bound to Florida
Upon a morn of autumn, crosses flying
The air-track of a snipe most passing fair—
Yet colder in her blood than she is fair—

And as that robin lingers on the wing,
And feels the snipe's flight in the eddying air,
And loves her for her coldness not the less—
But fain would win her to that warmer sky
Where love lies waking with the fragrant stars—
So I—a languisher for sunnier climes,
Where fruit, leaf, blossom, on the trees for ever
Image the tropic deathlessness of love—
Have met, and long'd to win thee, fairest lady,
To a more genial clime than cold Broadway !

Tranquil and effortless thou glidest on,
As doth the swan upon the yielding water,
And with a cheek like alabaster cold !
But as thou didst divide the amorous air
Just opposite the Astor, and didst lift
That veil of languid lashes to look in
At Leary's tempting window—lady ! then
My heart sprang in beneath that fringéd veil,
Like an adventurous bird that would escape
To some warm chamber from the outer cold !
And there would I delightedly remain,
And close that fringéd window with a kiss,
And in the warm sweet chamber of thy breast,
Be prisoner for ever !

LOVE IN A COTTAGE.

THEY may talk of love in a cottage,
  And bowers of trellised vine—
Of nature bewitchingly simple,
  And milkmaids half divine ;

They may talk of the pleasure of sleeping
  In the shade of a spreading tree,
And a walk in the fields at morning,
  By the side of a footstep free !

But give me a sly flirtation
  By the light of a chandelier—
With music to play in the pauses,
  And nobody very near ;
Or a seat on a silken sofa,
  With a glass of pure old wine,
And mamma too blind to discover
  The small white hand in mine.

Your love in a cottage is hungry,
  Your vine is a nest for flies—
Your milkmaid shocks the Graces,
  And simplicity talks of pies !
You lie down to your shady slumber,
  And wake with a bug in your ear,
And your damsel that walks in the morning
  Is shod like a mountaineer.

True love is at home on a carpet,
  And mightily likes his ease—
And true love has an eye for a dinner,
  And starves beneath shady trees.
His wing is the fan of a lady,
  His foot's an invisible thing,
And his arrow is tipp'd with a jewel,
  And shot from a silver string.

THE DECLARATION.

'TWAS late, and the gay company was gone,
And light lay soft on the deserted room
From alabaster vases, and a scent
Of orange leaves and sweet verbena came
Through the unshutter'd window on the air,
And the rich pictures with their dark old tints
Hung like a twilight landscape, and all things
Seem'd hush'd into a slumber.   Isabel,
The dark-eyed, spiritual Isabel,
Was leaning on her harp, and I had stay'd
To whisper what I could not when the crowd
Hung on her look like worshippers.   I knelt,
And with the fervour of a lip unused
To the cool breath of reason, told my love.
There was no answer, and I took the hand
That rested on the strings, and press'd a kiss
Upon it unforbidden—and again
Besought her, that this silent evidence
That I was not indifferent to her heart,
Might have the seal of one sweet syllable.
I kiss'd the small white fingers as I spoke,
And she withdrew them gently, and upraised
Her forehead from its resting-place, and look'd
Earnestly on me—*She had been asleep !*

MISCELLANEOUS POEMS.

MISCELLANEOUS POEMS.

PARRHASIUS.

"Parrhasius, a painter of Athens, among those Olynthian captives Philip of Macedon brought home to sell, bought one very old man; and when he had him at his house, put him to death with extreme torture and torment, the better, by his example, to express the pains and passions of his Prometheus, whom he was then about to paint."—*Burton's Anat. of Mel.*

THERE stood an unsold captive in the mart,
A grey-hair'd and majestical old man,
Chain'd to a pillar.   It was almost night,
And the last seller from his place had gone,
And not a sound was heard but of a dog
Crunching beneath the stall a refuse bone,
Or the dull echo from the pavement rung,
As the faint captive changed his weary feet.
He had stood there since morning, and had borne
From every eye in Athens the cold gaze
Of curious scorn.   The Jew had taunted him
For an Olynthian slave.   The buyer came
And roughly struck his palm upon his breast,
And touch'd his unheal'd wounds, and with a sneer
Pass'd on; and when, with weariness o'erspent,
He bow'd his head in a forgetful sleep,
Th' inhuman soldier smote him, and, with threats
Of torture to his children, summon'd back
The ebbing blood into his pallid face.

'Twas evening, and the half-descended sun
Tipp'd with a golden fire the many domes
Of Athens, and a yellow atmosphere
Lay rich and dusky in the shaded street
Through which the captive gazed.   He had borne up
With a stout heart that long and weary day,
Haughtily patient of his many wrongs,
But now he was alone, and from his nerves
The needless strength departed, and he lean'd
Prone on his massy chain, and let his thoughts
Throng on him as they would.   Unmark'd of him,
Parrhasius at the nearest pillar stood,
Gazing upon his grief.   Th' Athenian's cheek
Flush'd as he measured with a painter's eye
The moving picture.   The abandon'd limbs,
Stain'd with the oozing blood, were laced with veins
Swollen to purple fulness ; the grey hair,
Thin and disorder'd, hung about his eyes ;
And as a thought of wilder bitterness
Rose in his memory, his lips grew white,
And the fast workings of his bloodless face
Told what a tooth of fire was at his heart.

.   .   .   .   .   .

The golden light into the painter's room
Stream'd richly, and the hidden colours stole
From the dark pictures radiantly forth,
And in the soft and dewy atmosphere
Like forms and landscapes magical they lay.
The walls were hung with armour, and about
In the dim corners stood the sculptured forms
Of Cytheris, and Dian, and stern Jove,
And from the casement soberly away
Fell the grotesque long shadows, full and true,
And, like a veil of filmy mellowness,
The lint-spects floated in the twilight air.

Parrhasius stood, gazing forgetfully
Upon his canvas.   There Prometheus lay,
Chain'd to the cold rocks of Mount Caucasus—
The vulture at his vitals, and the links
Of the lame Lemnian festering in his flesh :
And, as the painter's mind felt through the dim,
Rapt mystery, and pluck'd the shadows forth
With its far-reaching fancy, and with form
And colour clad them, his fine, earnest eye,
Flash'd with a passionate fire, and the quick curl
Of his thin nostril, and his quivering lip
Were like the wing'd god's, breathing from his flight.

"Bring me the captive now !
My hand feels skilful, and the shadows lift
From my waked spirit airily and swift,
    And I could paint the bow
Upon the bended heavens—around me play
Colours of such divinity to-day.

"Ha ! bind him on his back !
Look !—as Prometheus in my picture here !
Quick—or he faints !—stand with the cordial near !
    Now—bend him to the rack !
Press down the poison'd links into his flesh ;
And tear agape that healing wound afresh !

"So—let him writhe !   How long
Will he live thus ?   Quick, my good pencil, now !
What a fine agony works upon his brow !
    Ha ! grey-hair'd, and so strong !
How fearfully he stifles that short moan !
Gods ! if I could but paint a dying groan !

"'Pity' thee !   So I do !
I pity the dumb victim at the altar—

But does the robed priest for his *pity* falter?
    I'd rack thee though I knew
A thousand lives were perishing in thine—
What were ten thousand to a fame like mine?

    "'Hereafter!' Ay—*hereafter!*
A whip to keep a coward to his track!
What gave Death ever from his kingdom back
    To check the sceptic's laughter?
Come from the grave to-morrow with that story—
And I may take some softer path to glory.

    "No, no, old man! we die
Even as the flowers, and we shall breathe away
Our life upon the chance wind, even as they!
    Strain well thy fainting eye—
For when that bloodshot quivering is o'er,
The light of heaven will never reach thee more.

    "Yet there's a deathless *name!*
A spirit that the smothering vault shall spurn,
And like a steadfast planet mount and burn—
    And though its crown of flame
Consumed my brain to ashes as it shone,
By all the fiery stars! I'd bind it on!

    "Ay—though it bid me rifle
My heart's last fount for its insatiate thirst—
Though every life-strung nerve be madden'd first—
    Though it should bid me stifle
The yearning in my throat for my sweet child,
And taunt its mother till my brain went wild—

    "All—I would do it all—
Sooner than die, like a dull worm, to rot—

Thrust foully into earth to be forgot!
   O heavens!—but I appal
Your heart, old man! forgive——ha! on your lives
Let him not faint!—rack him till he revives!

   "Vain—vain—give o'er! His eye
Glazes apace. He does not feel you now—
Stand back! I'll paint the death-dew on his brow!
   Gods! if he do not die
But for *one* moment—one—till I eclipse
Conception with the scorn of those calm lips!

   " Shivering! Hark! he mutters
Brokenly now—that was a difficult breath—
Another? Wilt thou never come, O Death!
   Look! how his temple flutters!
Is his heart still? Aha! lift up his head!
He shudders—gasps—Jove help him!—so—he's dead."

.   .   .   .   .

How like a mounting devil in the heart
Rules the unrein'd ambition! Let it once
But play the monarch, and its haughty brow
Glows with a beauty that bewilders thought
And unthrones peace for ever. Putting on
The very pomp of Lucifer, it turns
The heart to ashes, and with not a spring
Left in the bosom for the spirit's lip,
We look upon our splendour and forget
The thirst of which we perish! Yet hath life
Many a falser idol. There are hopes
Promising well; and love-touch'd dreams for some;
And passions, many a wild one; and fair schemes
For gold and pleasure—yet will only this
Balk not the soul—Ambition only, gives,
Even of bitterness, a beaker *full!*

Friendship is but a slow awaking dream,
Troubled at best—Love is a lamp unseen,
Burning to waste, or, if its light is found,
Nursed for an idle hour, then idly broken—
Gain is a grovelling care, and Folly tires,
And Quiet is a hunger never fed—
And from Love's very bosom, and from Gain,
Or Folly, or a Friend, or from Repose—
From all but keen Ambition—will the soul
Snatch the first moment of forgetfulness
To wander like a restless child away.
Oh, if there were not better hopes than these—
Were there no palm beyond a feverish fame—
If the proud wealth flung back upon the heart
Must canker in its coffers—if the links
Falsehood hath broken will unite no more—
If the deep-yearning love, that hath not found
Its like in the cold world, must waste in tears—
If truth, and fervour, and devotedness,
Finding no worthy altar, must return
And die of their own fulness—if beyond
The grave there is no heaven in whose wide air
The spirit may find room, and in the love
Of whose bright habitants the lavish heart
May spend itself—*what thrice-mock'd fools are we!*

*THE SCHOLAR OF THEBET BEN KHORAT.**

"Influentia cœli morbum hunc movet, interdum omnibus aliis amotis."
—*Melancthon de Anima, Cap. de Humoribus.*

I.

Night in Arabia. An hour ago,
Pale Dian had descended from the sky,
Flinging her cestus out upon the sea,
And at their watches, now, the solemn stars
Stood vigilant and lone; and, dead asleep,
With not a shadow moving on its breast,
The breathing earth lay in its silver dew,
And, trembling on their myriad viewless wings,
Th' imprison'd odours left the flowers to dream,
And stole away upon the yielding air.
Ben Khorat's tower stands shadowy and tall
In Mecca's loneliest street; and ever there,
When night is at the deepest, burns his lamp
As constant as the Cynosure, and forth
From his loop'd window stretch the brazen tubes,
Pointing for ever at the central star
Of that dim nebula just lifting now
Over Mount Arafat. The sky to-night
Is of a clearer blackness than is wont,
And far within its depths the coloured stars †

* A famous Arabian astrologer, who is said to have spent forty years in discovering the motion of the eighth sphere. He had a scholar, a young Bedouin Arab, who, with a singular passion for knowledge, abandoned his wandering tribe, and, applying himself too closely to astrology, lost his reason and died.

† "Even to the naked eye, the stars appear of palpably different colours; but when viewed with a prismatic glass, they may be very accurately classed into the red, the yellow, the brilliant white, the dull white, and the anomalous. This is true also of planets, which shine by reflected light, and of course the difference of colour must be supposed to arise from

N

Sparkle like gems—capricious Antares *
Flushing and paling in the southern arch ;
And azure Lyra, like a woman's eye,
Burning with soft blue lustre ; and away
Over the desert the bright polar star,
White as a flashing icicle ; and here,
Hung like a lamp, above th' Arabian sea,
Mars with his dusky glow ; and fairer yet,
Mild Sirius,† tinct with dewy violet,
Set like a flower upon the breast of Eve ;
And in the zenith the sweet Pleiades,‡
(Alas—that even a star may pass from heaven
And not be miss'd !)—the linkéd Pleiades
Undimm'd are there, though from the sister band
The fairest has gone down ; and, South away,
Hirundo § with its little company ;
And white-brow'd Vesta, lamping on her path
Lonely and planet-calm, and, all through heaven,
Articulate almost, they troop to-night,
Like unrobed angels in a prophet's trance.

Ben Khorat knelt before his telescope,‖
Gazing with earnest stillness on the stars.

their different powers to absorb and reflect the rays of the sun. The
original composition of the stars, and the different dispersive powers of
their different atmospheres, may be supposed to account also for this
phenomenon."

* This star exhibits a peculiar quality—a rapid and beautiful change
in the colour of its light ; every alternate twinkling being of an intense
reddish crimson colour, and the answering one of a brilliant white.

† When seen with a prismatic glass, Sirius shows a large brush of
exceedingly beautiful rays.

‡ The Pleiades are vertical in Arabia.

§ An Arabic constellation placed instead of the Piscis Australis, because
the swallow arrives in Arabia about the time of the heliacal rising of the
Fishes.

‖ An anachronism, the author is aware. The telescope was not invented
for a century or two after the time of Ben Khorat.

The grey hairs, struggling from his turban folds,
Play'd with the entering wind upon his cheeks,
And on his breast his venerable beard
With supernatural whiteness loosely fell.
The black flesh swell'd about his sandal-thongs,
Tight with his painful posture, and his lean
And wither'd fingers to his knees were clench'd
And the thin lashes of his straining eye
Lay with unwinking closeness to the lens,
Stiffen'd with tense up-turning.   Hour by hour,
Till the stars melted in the flush of morn,
The old astrologer knelt moveless there,
Ravish'd past pain with the bewildering spheres,
And, hour by hour, with the same patient thought,
Pored his pale scholar on the characters
Of Chaldee writ, or, as his gaze grew dim
With weariness, the dark-eyed Arab laid
His head upon the window and look'd forth
Upon the heavens awhile, until the dews
And the soft beauty of the silent night
Cool'd his flush'd eyelids, and then patiently
He turn'd unto his constant task again.

The sparry glinting of the Morning Star
Shot through the leaves of a majestic palm
Fringing Mount Arafat, and, as it caught
The eye of the rapt scholar, he arose
And clasp'd the volume with an eager haste,
And as the glorious planet mounted on,
Melting her way into the upper sky,
He breathlessly gazed on her :—

    " Star of the silver ray !
Bright as a god, but punctual as a slave—
What spirit the eternal canon gave
      That bends thee to thy way ?

What is the soul that, on thine arrowy light,
Is walking earth and heaven in pride to-night?

    " We know when thou wilt soar
Over the mount—thy change, and place, and time—
'Tis written in the Chaldee's mystic rhyme
    As 'twere a priceless lore!
I knew as much in my Bedouin garb—
Coursing the desert on my flying barb!

    " How oft amid the tents
Upon Sahara's sands I've walk'd alone,
Waiting all night for thee, resplendent one!
    With what magnificence,
In the last watches, to my thirsting eye,
Thy passionate beauty flush'd into the sky!

    " O God! how flew my soul
Out to thy glory—upward on thy ray—
Panting as thou ascendedst on thy way,
    As if thine own control—
This searchless spirit that I cannot find—
Had set its radiant law upon my mind!

    " More than all stars in heaven
I feel thee in my heart! my love became
A frenzy, and consumed me with its flame.
    Ay, in the desert even—
My dark-eyed Abra coursing at my side—
The star, not Abra, not my spirit's bride!

    " My Abra is no more!
My 'desert-bird' is in a stranger's stall—
My tribe, my tent—I sacrificed them all
    For this heart-wasting lore!—
Yet, than all these, the thought is sweeter far—
Thou wert ascendant at my birth, bright star!

" The Chaldee calls me *thine*—
And in this breast, that I must rend to be
A spirit upon wings of light like thee,
 I feel that *thou art mine !*
O God ! that these dull fetters would give way,
And let me forth to track thy silver ray ! "

      . . . Ben Khorat rose,
And silently look'd forth upon the east.
The dawn was stealing up into the sky
On its grey feet, the stars grew dim apace,
And faded, till the Morning Star alone,
Soft as a molten diamond's liquid fire,
Burn'd in the heavens. The morn grew freshlier—
The upper clouds were faintly touch'd with gold ;
The fan-palms rustled in the early air ;
Daylight spread cool and broadly to the hills ;
And still the star was visible, and still
The young Bedouin with a straining eye
Drank its departing light into his soul.
It faded—melted—and the fiery rim
Of the clear sun came up, and painfully
The passionate scholar press'd upon his eyes
His dusky fingers, and with limbs as weak
As a sick child's, turn'd fainting to his couch,
And slept. . . .

II.

. . It was the morning watch once more,
The clouds were drifting rapidly above,
And dim and fast the glimmering stars flew through ;
And as the fitful gush sough'd mournfully,
The shutters shook, and on the sloping roof
Plash'd, heavily, large, single drops of rain—
And all was still again. Ben Khorat sat
By the dim lamp, and, while his scholar slept,

Pored on the Chaldee wisdom.   At his feet,
Stretch'd on a pallet, lay the Arab boy,
Muttering fast in his unquiet sleep,
And working his dark fingers in his palms
Convulsively.   His sallow lips were pale,
And, as they moved, his teeth show'd ghastly through,
White as a charnel bone, and—closely drawn
Upon his sunken eyes, as if to press
Some frightful image from the bloodshot balls—
His lids a moment quiver'd, and again
Relax'd, half open, in a calmer sleep.
Ben Khorat gazed upon the drooping sands
Of the departing hour.   The last white grain
Fell through, and with the tremulous hand of age
The old astrologer reversed the glass;
And, as the voiceless monitor went on,
Wasting and wasting with the precious hour,
He look'd upon it with a moving lip,
And, starting, turn'd his gaze upon the heavens,
Cursing the clouds impatiently.

                              " 'Tis time !"
Mutter'd the dying scholar, and he dash'd
The tangled hair from his black eyes away,
And, seizing on Ben Khorat's mantle-folds,
He struggled to his feet, and falling prone
Upon the window-ledge, gazed steadfastly
Into the East :—

      " There is a cloud between—
She sits this instant on the mountain's brow,
And that dusk veil hides all her glory now—
      Yet floats she as serene
Into the heavens !——O God ! that even so
I could o'ermount *my* spirit-cloud, and go !

" The cloud begins to drift !
Aha ! fling open ! 'tis the star—the sky !
Touch me, immortal mother ! and I fly !
    Wider ! thou cloudy rift !
Let through !—such glory should have radiant room !
Let through !—a star-child on its light goes home !

" Speak to me, brethren bright !
Ye who are floating in these living beams !
Ye who have come to me in starry dreams !
    Ye who have wing'd the light
Of our bright mother with its thoughts of flame—
(I *knew* it pass'd through spirits as it came)—

"Tell me ! what power have ye ?
What are the heights ye reach upon your wings ?
What know ye of the myriad wondrous things
    I perish but to see ?
Are ye thought-rapid ?—Can ye fly as far—
As instant as a thought, from star to star ?

" Where has the Pleiad gone ?
Where have all missing stars* found light and home ?
Who bids the Stella Mira† go and come ?
    Why sits the Pole Star lone ?
And why, like banded sisters, through the air
Go in bright troops the constellations fair ?

* "Missing stars " are often spoken of in the old books of astronomy. Hipparchus mentions one that appeared and vanished very suddenly ; and in the beginning of the sixteenth century Kepler discovered a new star near the heel of the right foot of Serpentarius, "so bright and sparkling that it exceeded anything he had ever seen before." He "took notice that it was every moment changing into some of the colours of the rainbow, except when it was near the horizon, when it was generally white." It disappeared in the following year, and has not been seen since.

† A wonderful star in the neck of the Whale, discovered by Fabricius in the fifteenth century. It appears and disappears seven times in six years, and continues in the greatest lustre for fifteen days together.

" Ben Khorat ! dost thou mark ?
The star ! the star ! By heaven ! the cloud drifts o'er !
Gone—and I live ! nay—will my heart beat more ?
　　Look ! master ! 'tis all dark !
Not a clear speck in heaven !—my eyeballs smother !
Break through the clouds once more ! O starry mother !

" I will lie down ! Yet stay,
The rain beats out the odour from the gums,
And strangely soft to-night the spice-wind comes !
　　I am a child alway
When it is on my forehead ! Abra sweet !
Would I were in the desert at thy feet !

" My barb ! my glorious steed !
Methinks my soul would mount upon its track
More fleetly, could I die upon thy back !
　　How would thy thrilling speed
Quicken my pulse !—O Allah ! I get wild !
Would that I were once more a desert-child !

" Nay—nay—I had forgot !
My mother ! my starry mother !—Ha ! my breath
Stifles——more air !——Ben Khorat ! this is—death !
　　Touch me !——I feel you not !
Dying !—Farewell ! good master !—room ! more room !
Abra ! I loved thee ! star ! bright star ! I—— come ! "

How idly of the human heart we speak,
Giving it gods of clay ! How worse than vain
Is the school homily, that Eden's fruit
Cannot be pluck'd too freely from " the tree
Of good and evil." Wisdom sits alone,
Topmost in heaven ;—she is its light—its God !
And in the heart of man she sits as high—
Though grovelling eyes forget her oftentimes,

Seeing but this world's idols. The pure mind
Sees her for ever : and in youth we come
Filled with her sainted ravishment, and kneel,
Worshipping God through her sweet altar-fires,
And then is knowledge " good." We come too oft—
The heart grows proud with fulness, and we soon
Look with licentious freedom on the maid
Throned in celestial beauty. There she sits,
Robed in her soft and seraph loveliness,
Instructing and forgiving, and we gaze
Until desire grows wild, and, with our hands
Upon her very garments, are struck down,
Blasted with a consuming fire from heaven !
Yet, oh ! how full of music from her lips
Breathe the calm tones of wisdom ! Human praise
Is sweet—till envy mars it, and the touch
Of new-won gold stirs up the pulses well ;
And woman's love, if in a beggar's lamp
'Twould burn, might light us clearly through the world ;
But Knowledge hath a far more 'wildering tongue,
And she will stoop and lead you to the stars,
And witch you with her mysteries—till gold
Is a forgotten dross, and power and fame
Toys of an hour, and woman's careless love,
Light as the breath that breaks it. He who binds
His soul to knowledge steals the key of heaven—
But 'tis a bitter mockery that the fruit
May hang within his reach, and when, with thirst
Wrought to a maddening frenzy, he would taste—
It burns his lips to ashes !

———

THE DYING ALCHYMIST.

THE night wind with a desolate moan swept by;
And the old shutters of the turret swung
Screaming upon their hinges; and the moon,
As the torn edges of the clouds flew past,
Struggled aslant the stain'd and broken panes
So dimly, that the watchful eye of death
Scarcely was conscious when it went and came.

. . . .

The fire beneath the crucible was low;
Yet still it burn'd; and ever as his thoughts
Grew insupportable, he raised himself
Upon his wasted arm, and stirr'd the coals
With difficult energy; and when the rod
Fell from his nerveless fingers, and his eye
Felt faint within its socket, he shrunk back
Upon his pallet, and with unclosed lips
Mutter'd a curse on death! The silent room,
From its dim corners mockingly gave back
His rattling breath; the humming in the fire
Had the distinctness of a knell; and when
Duly the antique horologe beat one,
He drew a phial from beneath his head,
And drank. And instantly his lips compress'd,
And, with a shudder in his skeleton frame,
He rose with supernatural strength, and sat
Upright, and communed with himself:—

" I did not think to die
Till I had finish'd what I had to do;
I thought to pierce th' eternal secret through
    With this my mortal eye;
I felt—O God! it seemeth even now
This cannot be the death-dew on my brow!

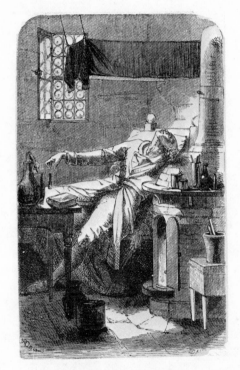

THE DYING ALCHYMIST. P. 203.

" And yet it is—I feel,
Of this dull sickness at my heart, afraid !
And in my eyes the death-sparks flash and fade ;
   And something seems to steal
Over my bosom like a frozen hand—
Binding its pulses with an icy band.

   " And this is death !   But why
Feel I this wild recoil ?   It cannot be
Th' immortal spirit shuddereth to be free !
   Would it not leap to fly,
Like a chain'd eaglet at its parent's call ?
I fear—I fear—that this poor life is all !

   " Yet thus to pass away !—
To live but for a hope that mocks at last—
To agonise, to strive, to watch, to fast,
   To waste the light of day,
Night's better beauty, feeling, fancy, thought,
All that we have and are—for this—for naught !

   " Grant me another year,
God of my spirit !—but a day—to win
Something to satisfy this thirst within !
   I would *know* something here !
Break for me but one seal that is unbroken !
Speak for me but one word that is unspoken !

   " Vain—vain !—my brain is turning
With a swift dizziness, and my heart grows sick,
And these hot temple-throbs come fast and thick,
   And I am freezing—burning—
Dying !   O God ! if I might only live !
My phial———Ha ! it thrills me—I revive !

.   .   .   .   .   .

" Ay—were not man to die,
He were too mighty for this narrow sphere !
Had he but time to brood on knowledge here—
 Could he but train his eye—
Might he but wait the mystic word and hour—
Only his Maker would transcend his power !

" Earth has no mineral strange—
Th' illimitable air no hidden wings—
Water no quality in covert springs,
 And fire no power to change—
Seasons no mystery, and stars no spell,
Which the unwasting soul might not compel.

" Oh, but for time to track
The upper stars into the pathless sky—
To see th' invisible spirits, eye to eye—
 To hurl the lightning back—
To tread unhurt the sea's dim-lighted halls—
To chase Day's chariot to the horizon walls—

" And more, much more—for now
The life-seal'd fountains of my nature move—
To nurse and purify this human love—
 To clear the godlike brow
Of weakness and mistrust, and bow it down,
Worthy and beautiful, to the much-loved one—

" This were indeed to feel
The soul-thirst slaken at the living stream—
To live—O God ! that life is but a dream !
 And death——Aha ! I reel—
Dim—dim—I faint—darkness comes o'er my eye—
Cover me ! save me !——God of heaven ! I die !"

'Twas morning, and the old man lay alone.
No friend had closed his eyelids, and his lips,

Open and ashy pale, th' expression wore
Of his death-struggle.   His long silvery hair
Lay on his hollow temples thin and wild,
His frame was wasted, and his features wan
And haggard as with want, and in his palm
His nails were driven deep, as if the throe
Of the last agony had wrung him sore.
The storm was raging still.   The shutters swung
Screaming as harshly in the fitful wind,
And all without went on—as aye it will,
Sunshine or tempest, reckless that a heart
Is breaking, or has broken, in its change.

The fire beneath the crucible was out ;
The vessels of his mystic art lay round,
Useless and cold as the ambitious hand
That fashion'd them, and the small rod,
Familiar to his touch for threescore years,
Lay on th' alembic's rim, as if it still
Might vex the elements at its master's will.

And thus had pass'd from its unequal frame
A soul of fire—a sun-bent eagle stricken
From his high soaring down—an instrument
Broken with its own compass.   Oh how poor
Seems the rich gift of genius, when it lies,
Like the adventurous bird that hath out-flown
His strength upon the sea, ambition-wreck'd—
A thing the thrush might pity, as she sits
Brooding in quiet in her lowly nest !

TO ERMENGARDE.

I KNOW not if the sunshine waste—
　　The world is dark since thou art gone!
The hours are, oh! so leaden-paced!
　　The birds sing, and the stars float on,
But sing not well, and look not fair—
A weight is in the summer air,
　　And sadness in the sight of flowers;
And if I go where others smile,
　　Their love but makes me think of ours,
And heavier gets my heart the while.
Like one upon a desert isle,
　　I languish of the weary hours;
I never thought a life *could* be
So flung upon one hope, as mine, dear love, on thee!

I sit and watch the summer sky.
　　There comes a cloud through heaven alone;
A thousand stars are shining nigh—
　　It feels no light, but darkles on!
Yet now it nears the lovelier moon;
　　And, flushing through its fringe of snow,
There steals a rosier dye, and soon
　　Its bosom is one fiery glow!
The Queen of Light within it lies!
　　Yet mark how lovers meet to part!
The cloud already onward flies,
　　And shadows sink into its heart,
And (dost thou see them where thou art?)
　　Fade fast, fade all those glorious dyes!
Its light, like mine, is seen no more,
And, like my own, its heart seems darker than before!

Where press this hour those fairy feet ?
　　Where look this hour those eyes of blue ?
What music in thine ear is sweet ?
　　What odour breathes thy lattice through ?
What word is on thy lip ? what tone—
What look—replying to thine own ?
Thy steps along the Danube stray—
　　Alas ! it seeks an orient sea !
Thou wouldst not seem so far away
　　Flow'd but its waters back to me !
I bless the slowly coming moon
　　Because its eye look'd late in thine !
I envy the west wind of June
　　Whose wings will bear it up the Rhine ;
The flower I press upon my brow
Were sweeter if its like perfumed thy chamber now !

————

MELANIE.

I.

I STOOD on yonder rocky brow,*
　　And marvell'd at the Sibyl's fane,
When I was not what I am now.
　　My life was then untouch'd of pain ;
And, as the breeze that stirr'd my hair,
　　My spirit freshen'd in the sky,
And all things that were true and fair
　　Lay closely to my loving eye,
With nothing shadowy between—
I was a boy of seventeen.

* The story is told during a walk around the Cascatelles of Tivoli.

Yon wondrous temple crests the rock—
　As light upon its giddy base,
As stirless with the torrent's shock,
　As pure in its proportion'd grace,
And seems a thing of air—as then,
Afloat above this fairy glen ;
　But though mine eye will kindle still
In looking on the shapes of art,
　The link is lost that sent the thrill,
Like lightning instant to my heart.
And thus may break, before we die,
Th' electric chain 'twixt soul and eye !

Ten years—like yon bright valley, sown
　Alternately with weeds and flowers—
Had swiftly, if not gaily, flown,
　And still I loved the rosy hours ;
And if there lurk'd within my breast
　Some nerve that had been overstrung
And quiver'd in my hours of rest,
　Like bells by their own echo rung,
I was with Hope a masquer yet,
　And well could hide the look of sadness ;
And, if my heart would not forget,
　I knew, at least, the trick of gladness ;
And when another sang the strain,
I mingled in the old refrain.

'Twere idle to remember now,
　Had I the heart, my thwarted schemes.
I bear beneath this alter'd brow
　The ashes of a thousand dreams—
Some wrought of wild Ambition's fingers,
　Some colour'd of Love's pencil well—
But none of which a shadow lingers,
　And none whose story I could tell.

Enough, that when I climb'd again
   To Tivoli's romantic steep,
Life had no joy, and scarce a pain,
   Whose wells I had not tasted deep;
And from my lips the thirst had pass'd
For every fount save one—the sweetest, and the last.

The last—the last! My friends were dead,
   Or false; my mother in her grave;
Above my father's honour'd head
   The sea had lock'd its hiding wave;
Ambition had but foil'd my grasp,
And love had perish'd in my clasp;
   And still, I say, I did not slack
My love of life, and hope of pleasure,
   But gather'd my affections back;
And, as the miser hugs his treasure
   When plague and ruin bid him flee,
I closer clung to mine—my loved, lost Melanie!

The last of the De Brevern race,
   My sister claim'd no kinsman's care;
And, looking from each other's face,
   The eye stole upward unaware—
For there was naught whereon to lean
Each other's heart and heaven between—
   Yet that was world enough for me;
And, for a brief but blessed while,
   There seem'd no care for Melanie
If she could see her brother smile!
   But life with her was at the flow,
And every wave went sparkling higher,
   While mine was ebbing, fast and low,
From the same shore of vain desire;
   And knew I, with prophetic heart,
That we were wearing, aye, insensibly apart.

o

II.

We came to Italy.   I felt
   A yearning for its sunny sky;
My very spirit seem'd to melt
   As swept its first warm breezes by.
From lip and cheek a chilling mist,
   From life and soul a frozen rime,
By every breath seem'd softly kiss'd—
   God's blessing on its radiant clime!
It was an endless joy to me
   To see my sister's new delight;
From Venice in its golden sea
   To Pœstum in its purple light—
By sweet Val d'Arno's tinted hills—
   In Vallombrosa's convent gloom—
'Mid Terni's vale of singing rills—
   By deathless lairs in solemn Rome—
In gay Palermo's "Golden Shell"—
   At Arethusa's hidden well—
We loiter'd like th' impassion'd sun,
That slept so lovingly on all,
   And made a home of every one—
Ruin, and fane, and waterfall—
   And crown'd the dying day with glory
If we had seen, since morn, but one old haunt of story.

We came with Spring to Tivoli.
   My sister loved its laughing air
And merry waters, though, for me,
   My heart was in another key;
   And sometimes I could scarcely bear
The mirth of their eternal play,
   And, like a child that longs for home

When weary of its holiday,
   I sigh'd for melancholy Rome.
Perhaps—the fancy haunts me still—
'Twas but a boding sense of ill.

It was a morn of such a day
   As might have dawn'd on Eden first,
Early in the Italian May.
   Vine-leaf and flower had newly burst,
And on the burthen of the air
The breath of buds faint and rare;
   And far in the transparent sky
The small, earth-keeping birds were seen
   Soaring deliriously high;
And through the clefts of newer green
   Yon waters dash'd their living pearls;
And with a gayer smile and bow
   Troop'd on the merry village-girls;
And from the Contadino's brow
   The low-slouch'd hat was backward thrown,
   With air that scarcely seem'd his own;
And Melanie, with lips apart,
   And claspéd hands upon my arm,
Flung open her impassion'd heart,
   And bless'd life's mere and breathing charm;
And sang old songs, and gather'd flowers,
And passionately bless'd once more life's thrilling hours.

In happiness and idleness
   We wander'd down yon sunny vale—
Oh mocking eyes!—a golden tress
   Floats back upon this summer gale!
A foot is tripping on the grass!
   A laugh rings merry in mine ear!
I see a bounding shadow pass!—
   O God! my sister *once* was here!

Come with me, friend!—We rested yon!
  There grew a flower she pluck'd and wore!
She sat upon this mossy stone—
  That broken fountain running o'er
With the same ring, like silver bells.
  She listen'd to its babbling flow,
And said, "Perhaps the gossip tells
  Some fountain-nymph's love-story now."
And as her laugh rang clear and wild,
A youth—a painter—pass'd and smiled.

He gave the greeting of the morn
  With voice that linger'd in mine ear.
I knew him sad and gentle born
  By those two words—so calm and clear.
His frame was slight, his forehead high,
  And swept by threads of raven hair,
The fire of thought was in his eye,
  And he was pale and marble fair,
And Grecian chisel never caught
The soul in those slight features wrought.
  I watch'd his graceful step of pride,
Till hidden by yon leaning tree,
  And loved him ere the echo died;
And so, alas! did Melanie!

We sat and watch'd the fount awhile
  In silence, but our thoughts were one;
And then arose, and, with a smile
  Of sympathy, we saunter'd on;
And she by sudden fits was gay,
And then her laughter died away.
  And in this changefulness of mood,
(Forgotten now those May-day spells,)
  We turn'd where Varro's villa stood,
And gazing on the Cascatelles,

(Whose hurrying waters wild and white
   Seem madden'd as they burst to light,)
I chanced to turn my eyes away,
   And lo! upon a bank, alone,
The youthful painter, sleeping, lay!

   His pencils on the grass were thrown,
And by his side a sketch was flung,
   And near him as I lightly crept,
   To see the picture as he slept,
Upon his feet he lightly sprung;

   And, gazing with a wild surprise
Upon the face of Melanie,
   He said—and dropp'd his earnest eyes—
"Forgive me! but I dream'd of thee!"

   His sketch, the while, was in my hand,
And, for the lines I look'd to trace—
   A torrent by a palace spann'd,
   Half classic and half fairy-land—
I only found—my sister's face!

III.

Our life was changed. Another love
   In its lone woof began to twine;
But ah! the golden thread was wove
   Between my sister's heart and mine!
She who had lived for me before—

   She who had smiled for me alone—
Would live and smile for me no more!
   The echo to my heart was gone!
It seem'd to me the very skies
Had shone through those averted eyes;

   The air had breathed of balm—the flower
Of radiant beauty seem'd to be—
   But as *she* loved them, hour by hour,
And murmur'd of that love to *me!*

Oh, though it be so heavenly high
   The selfishness of earth above,
That, of the watchers in the sky,
   He sleeps who guards a brother's love—
Though to a sister's present weal
   The deep devotion far transcends
The utmost that the soul can feel
   For even its own higher ends—
Though next to God, and more than heaven
For his own sake, he loves her, even—
   'Tis difficult to see another,
A passing stranger of a day,
   Who never hath been friend or brother,
Pluck with a look her heart away—
   To see the fair, unsullied brow,
Ne'er kiss'd before without a prayer,
   Upon a stranger's bosom now,
Who for the boon took little care—
   Who is enrich'd, he knows not why—
Who suddenly hath found a treasure
   Golconda were too poor to buy,
And he, perhaps, too cold to measure—
(Albeit, in her forgetful dream,
Th' unconscious idol happier seem,)
   'Tis difficult at once to crush
The rebel mourner in the breast,
   To press the heart to earth, and hush
Its bitter jealousy to rest—
   And difficult—the eye gets dim,
   The lip wants power—to smile on *him!*

I thank sweet Mary Mother now,
   Who gave me strength those pangs to hide—
And touch'd mine eyes and lit my brow
   With sunshine that my heart belied.

I never spoke of wealth or race
    To one who ask'd so much from me—
I look'd but in my sister's face,
    And mused if she would happier be ;
And hour by hour, and day by day,
    I loved the gentle painter more,
    And, in the same soft measure, wore
My selfish jealousy away ;
    And I began to watch his mood,
And fear, with her, love's trembling care,
    And bade God bless him as he woo'd
That loving girl so fond and fair.
    And on my mind would sometimes press
    A fear that she might love him less.

But Melanie—I little dream'd
    What spells the stirring heart may move—
Pygmalion's statue never seem'd
    More changed with life, than she with love !
The pearl-tint of the early dawn
    Flush'd into day-spring's rosy hue—
The meek, moss-folded bud of morn
    Flung open to the light and dew—
The first and half-seen star of even
Wax'd clear amid the deepening heaven—
    Similitudes perchance may be !
But these are changes oftener seen,
    And do not image half to me
My sister's change of face and mien.
    'Twas written in her very air
    That Love had pass'd and enter'd there.

IV.

A calm and lovely paradise
    Is Italy, for minds at ease.

The sadness of its sunny skies
   Weighs not upon the lives of these.
The ruin'd aisle, the crumbling fane,
   The broken column, vast and prone—
It may be joy—it may be pain—
   Amid such wrecks to walk alone !
The saddest man will sadder be,
   The gentlest lover gentler there—
As if, whate'er the spirit's key,
   It strengthen'd in that solemn air.

The heart soon grows to mournful things,
   And Italy has not a breeze
But comes on melancholy wings;
   And even her majestic trees
Stand ghostlike in the Cæsars' home,
   As if their conscious roots were set
In the old graves of giant Rome,
   And drew their sap all kingly yet !
And every stone your feet beneath
   Is broken from some mighty thought ;
And sculptures in the dust still breathe
   The fire with which their lines were wrought ;
And sunder'd arch, and plunder'd tomb,
Still thunder back the echo, " Rome ! "

Yet, gaily o'er Egeria's fount
   The ivy flings its emerald veil,
And flowers grow fair on Numa's mount,
   And light-sprung arches span the dale ;
And soft, from Caracalla's baths,
   The herdsman's song comes down the breeze,
While climb his goats the giddy paths
   To grass-grown architrave and frieze,
And gracefully Albano's hill
   Curves into the horizon's line ;

And sweetly sings that classic rill;
    And fairly stands that nameless shrine;
And here, oh, many a sultry noon
And starry eve, that happy June,
    Came Angelo and Melanie!
And earth for us was all in tune—
For while Love talk'd with them, Hope walk'd apart
    with me!

v.

I shrink from the embitter'd close
    Of my own melancholy tale.
'Tis long since I have waked my woes—
    And nerve and voice together fail!
The throb beats faster at my brow,
    My brain feels warm with starting tears,
And I shall weep—but heed not thou!
    'Twill soothe awhile the ache of years!
The heart transfix'd—worn out with grief—
Will turn the arrow for relief.

The painter was a child of shame!
    It stirr'd my pride to know it first,
For I had question'd but his name,
    And thought, alas! I knew the worst,
Believing him unknown and poor.
His blood, indeed, was not obscure;
    A high-born Conti was his mother,
But, though he knew one parent's face,
    He never had beheld the other,
Nor knew his country or his race.
    The Roman hid his daughter's shame
Within St. Mona's convent wall,
    And gave the boy a painter's name—
And little else to live withal!

And, with a noble's high desires
For ever mounting in his heart,
   The boy consumed with hidden fires,
But wrought in silence at his art;
   And sometimes at St. Mona's shrine,
Worn thin with penance harsh and long,
   He saw his mother's form divine,
And loved her for their mutual wrong.
   I said my pride was stirr'd—but no!
The voice that told its bitter tale
   Was touch'd so mournfully with woe,
And, as he ceased, all deathly pale,
   He loosed the hand of Melanie,
   And gazed so gaspingly on me—
The demon in my bosom died!
" Not thine," I said, " another's guilt;
   I break no hearts for silly pride;
So, kiss yon weeper if thou wilt ! "

VI.

St. Mona's morning mass was done,
   The shrine-lamps struggled with the day;
And rising slowly, one by one,
   Stole the last worshippers away.
The organist play'd out the hymn,
   The incense, to St. Mary swung,
Had mounted to the cherubim,
   Or to the pillars thinly clung;
And boyish chorister replaced
   The missal that was read no more,
And closed, with half irreverent haste,
   Confessional and chancel door;
And as, through aisle and oriel pane,
   The sun wore round his slanting beam,

The dying martyr stirr'd again,
    And warriors battled in its gleam;
And costly tomb and sculptured knight
Show'd warm and wondrous in the light.
    I have not said that Melanie
        Was radiantly fair—
This earth again may never see
    A loveliness so rare!
She glided up St. Mona's aisle
    That morning as a bride,
And, full as was my heart the while,
    I bless'd her in my pride!
The fountain may not fail the less
    Whose sands are golden ore,
And a sister for her loveliness,
    May not be loved the more;
But as, the fount's full heart beneath,
    Those golden sparkles shine,
My sister's beauty seem'd to breathe
    Its brightness over mine!

St. Mona has a chapel dim
    Within the altar's fretted pale,
Where faintly comes the swelling hymn,
    And dies, half lost, the anthem's wail.
And here, in twilight meet for prayer,
    A single lamp hangs o'er the shrine,
And Raphael's Mary, soft and fair,
    Looks down with sweetness half divine,
And here St. Mona's nuns alway
Through latticed bars are seen to pray.

Avé and sacrament were o'er,
    And Angelo and Melanie
Still knelt the holy shrine before;
    But prayer that morn was not for me!

My heart was lock'd! The lip might stir,
　　The frame might agonize—and yet,
O God! I could not pray for *her!*
　　A seal upon my brow was set—
My brow was hot—my brain oppress'd—
And fiends seem'd muttering round, "Your bridal is
　　unblest!"

With forehead to the lattice laid,
　　And thin, white fingers straining through,
A nun the while had softly pray'd.
　　Oh, even in prayer that voice I knew!
Each faltering word—each mournful tone—
　　Each pleading cadence, half suppress'd—
Such music had its like alone
　　On lips that stole it at her breast!
And ere the orison was done
I loved the mother as the son!

And now, the marriage vows to hear,
　　The nun unveil'd her brow—
When, sudden, to my startled ear,
There crept a whisper, hoarse like fear,
　　" *De Brevern! is it thou!* "
The priest let fall the golden ring,
　　The bridegroom stood aghast,
While, like some weird and frantic thing,
　　The nun was muttering fast ;
And as, in dread, I nearer drew,
She thrust her arms the lattice through,

And held me to her straining view—
　　But suddenly begun
To steal upon her brain a light
That stagger'd soul, and sense, and sight,
And, with a mouth all ashy white,
　　She shriek'd, " *It is his son!*

The bridegroom is thy blood—thy brother!
Rodolph de Brevern wrong'd his mother!"
    And, as that doom of love was heard,
My sister sunk—and died—without a sign or word!

  .   .   .   .   .   .

  I shed no tear for her. She died
    With her last sunshine in her eyes.
Earth held for her no joy beside
    The hope just shatter'd—and she lies
In a green nook of yonder dell;
    And near her, in a newer bed,
Her lover—brother—sleeps as well!
  Peace to the broken-hearted dead!

———

THE DEATH OF HARRISON.

WHAT! soar'd the old eagle to die at the sun!
Lies he stiff with spread wings at the goal he had won!
Are there spirits more blest than the "Planet of Even,"
Who mount to their zenith, then melt into heaven—
No waning of fire, no quenching of ray,
But rising, still rising, when passing away?
Farewell, gallant eagle! thou'rt buried in light!
God-speed into heaven, lost star of our night!

Death! Death in the White House! Ah, never before,
Trod his skeleton foot on the President's floor!
He is look'd for in hovel, and dreaded in hall—
The king in his closet keeps hatchment and pall—
The youth in his birth-place, the old man at home,
Make clean from the door-stone the path to the tomb;—
But the lord of this mansion was cradled not here—
In a churchyard far off stands his beckoning bier!
He is here as the wave-crest heaves flashing on high—
As the arrow is stopp'd by its prize in the sky—

The arrow to earth, and the foam to the shore—
Death finds them when swiftness and sparkle are o'er—
But Harrison's death fills the climax of story—
He went with his old stride—from glory to glory !

Lay his sword on his breast ! There's no spot on its blade
In whose cankering breath his bright laurels will fade !
'Twas the first to lead on at humanity's call—
It was stay'd with sweet mercy when " glory " was all !
As calm in the council as gallant in war,
He fought for his country, and not its " hurrah ! "
In the path of the hero with pity he trod—
Let him pass, with his sword, to the presence of God !

What more ? Shall we on, with his ashes ? Yet stay !
He hath ruled the wide realm of a king in his day !
At his word, like a monarch's, went treasure and land—
The bright gold of thousands has pass'd thro' his hand—
Is there nothing to show of his glittering hoard ?
No jewel to deck the rude hilt of his sword—
No trappings—no horses ?— what had he but now ?
On !—on with his ashes !—HE LEFT BUT HIS PLOUGH !
Brave old Cincinnatus ! Unwind ye his sheet !
Let him sleep as he lived—with his purse *at his feet !*

Follow now, as ye list ! The first mourner to-day
Is the nation—whose father is taken away !
Wife, children, and neighbour, may moan at his knell—
He was " lover and friend " to his country, as well !
For the stars on our banner, grown suddenly dim,
Let us weep, in our darkness—but weep not for him !
Not for him—who, departing, leaves millions in tears !
Not for him—who has died full of honour and years !
Not for him—who ascended Fame's ladder so high !
From the round at the top he has stepp'd to the sky !

ANDRE'S REQUEST TO WASHINGTON.

It is not the fear of death
   That damps my brow,
It is not for another breath
   I ask thee now ;
I can die with a lip unstirr'd,
   And a quiet heart—
Let but this prayer be heard
   Ere I depart.

I can give up my mother's look—
   My sister's kiss ;
I can think of love—yet brook
   A death like this !
I can give up the young fame
   I burn'd to win—
All—but the spotless name
   I glory in.

Thine is the power to give,
   Thine to deny,
Joy for the hour I live—
   Calmness to die.
By all the brave should cherish,
   By my dying breath,
I ask that I may perish
   By a soldier's death !

LORD IVON AND HIS DAUGHTER.

> "Dost thou despise
> A love like *this?* A lady should not scorn
> One soul that loves her, howe'er lowly it be."

LORD IVON.

How beautiful it is ! Come here, my daughter !
Is it not a face of much bewildering brightness ?

ISIDORE.

The features are all fair, sir, but so cold—
I could not love such beauty !

LORD IVON.

               Yet, e'en so
Look'd thy lost mother, Isidore !   Her brow
Lofty like this—her lips thus delicate,
Yet icy cold in their slight vermeil threads—
Her neck thus queenly, and the sweeping curve
Thus matchless, from the small and "pearl round ear
To the o'er-polish'd shoulder.   Never swan
Dream'd on the water with a grace so calm !

ISIDORE.

And was she proud, sir ?

LORD IVON.

               Or I had not loved her.

ISIDORE.

Then runs my lesson wrong.   I ever read
Pride was unlovely.

LORD IVON.

       Dost thou prate already
Of books, my little one ? Nay, then, 'tis time
That a sad tale were told thee. Is thy bird
Fed for the day ? Canst thou forget the rein
Of thy beloved Arabian for an hour,
And, the first time in all thy sunny life,
Take sadness to thy heart ? Wilt listen, sweet ?

ISIDORE.

Hang I not ever on thy lips, dear father ?

LORD IVON.

As thou didst enter, I was musing here
Upon this picture. 'Tis the face of one
I never knew ; but, for its glorious pride,
I bought it of the painter. There has hung
Ever the cunning curse upon my soul
To love this look in woman. Not the flower
Of all Arcadia, in the Age of Gold,
Look'd she a shepherdess, would be to me
More than the birds are. As th' astrologer
Worships the half-seen star that in its sphere
Dreams not of him, and tramples on the lily
That flings, unask'd, its fragrance in his way,
Yet both (as are the high-born and the low)
Wrought of the same fine Hand—so, daringly,
Flew my boy-hopes beyond me. You are here
In a brave palace, Isidore ! The gem
That sparkles on your hair imprisons light
Drunk in the flaming Orient ; and gold
Waits on the bidding of those girlish lips
In measure that Aladdin never knew.
Yet was I—lowly born !

P

ISIDORE.

Lord Ivon !

LORD IVON.

Ay,

You wonder ; but I tell you that the lord
Of this tall palace was a peasant's child !
And, looking sometimes on his fair domain,
Thy sire bethinks him of a sickly boy,
Nursed by his mother on a mountain side,
His only wealth a book of poetry,
With which he daily crept into the sun,
To cheat sharp pains with the bewildering dream
Of beauty he had only read of there.

ISIDORE.

Have you the volume still, sir ?

LORD IVON.

'Twas the gift
Of a poor scholar wandering in the hills,
Who pitied my sick idleness.   I fed
My inmost soul upon the witching rhyme —
A silly tale of a low minstrel boy,
Who broke his heart in singing for a bridal.

ISIDORE.

Loved he the lady, sir ?

LORD IVON.

So ran the tale.
How well do I remember it !

ISIDORE.

Alas !

Poor youth !

LORD IVON.

I never thought to *pity* him.
The bride was a duke's sister; and I mused
Upon the wonder of his daring love,
Till my heart changed within me.   I became
Restless and sad; and in my sleep I saw
Beautiful dames all scornfully go by;
And one o'er-weary morn I crept away
Into the glen, and, flung upon a rock,
Over a torrent whose swift, giddy waters
Fill'd me with energy, I swore my soul
To better that false vision, if there were
Manhood or fire within my wretched frame.
I turn'd me homeward with the sunset hour,
Changed—for the thought had conquer'd even disease;
And my poor mother check'd her busy wheel
To wonder at the step with which I came.

Oh, heavens! that soft and dewy April eve,
When, in a minstrel's garb, but with a heart
As lofty as the marble shafts uprear'd
Beneath the stately portico, I stood
At this same palace door!

ISIDORE.

     Our own! and you
A minstrel boy!

LORD IVON.

     Yes—I had wander'd far
Since I shook off my sickness in the hills,
And, with some cunning on the lute, had learn'd
A subtler lesson than humility
In the quick school of want.   A menial stood
By the Egyptian sphinx; and when I came
And pray'd to sing beneath the balcony

A song of love for a fair lady's ear,
He insolently bade me to be gone.
Listening not, I swept my fingers o'er
The strings in prelude, when the base-born slave
Struck me!

ISIDORE.

Impossible!

LORD IVON.

                I dash'd my lute
Into his face, and o'er the threshold flew;
And threading rapidly the loftly rooms,
Sought vainly for his master. Suddenly
A wing rush'd o'er me, and a radiant girl,
Young as myself, but fairer than the dream
Of my most wild imagining, sprang forth,
Chasing a dove, that, 'wilder'd with pursuit,
Dropp'd breathless on my bosom.

ISIDORE.

                        Nay, dear father!
Was't so indeed?

LORD IVON.

                I thank'd my blessed star!
And, as the fair, transcendent creature stood
Silent with wonder, I resign'd the bird
To her white hands: and, with a rapid thought,
And lips already eloquent of love,
Turn'd the strange chance to a similitude
Of my own story. Her slight, haughty lip
Curl'd at the warm recital of my wrong,
And on the ivory oval of her cheek
The rose flush'd outward with a deeper red;
And from that hour the minstrel was at home,
And horse and hound were his, and none might cross

The minion of the noble Lady Clare.
Art weary of my tale ?

ISIDORE.

Dear father !

LORD IVON.

Well !

A summer, and a winter, and a spring,
Went over me like brief and noteless hours.
For ever at the side of one who grew
With every morn more beautiful ; the slave,
Willing and quick, of every idle whim ;
Singing for no one's bidding but her own,
And then a song from my own passionate heart,
Sung with a lip of fire, but ever named
As an old rhyme that I had chanced to hear ;
Riding beside her, sleeping at her door,
Doing her maddest bidding at the risk
Of life—what marvel if at last I grew
Presumptuous ?

A messenger one morn
Spurr'd through the gate—"A revel at the court !
And many minstrels, come from many lands,
Will try their harps in presence of the king ;
And 'tis the royal pleasure that my lord
Come with the young and lovely Lady Clare,
Robed as the queen of Faery, who shall crown
The victor with his bays."

Pass over all
To that bewildering day.   She sat enthroned
Amid the court ; and never twilight star
Sprang with such sweet surprise upon the eye,
As she with her rare beauty on the gaze

Of the gay multitude.　The minstrels changed
Their studied songs, and chose her for a theme;
And ever at the pause all eyes upturn'd
And fed upon her loveliness.

　　　　　　　　　The last
Long lay was ended, and the silent crowd
Waited the king's award—when suddenly
The sharp strings of a lyre were swept without,
And a clear voice claimed hearing for a bard
Belated on his journey.　Mask'd, and clad
In a long stole, the herald led me in.
A thousand eyes were on me: but I saw
The new-throned queen, in her high place, alone;
And, kneeling at her feet, I press'd my brow
Upon her footstool, till the images
Of my past hours rush'd thick upon my brain;
Then, rising hastily, I struck my lyre;
And, in a story woven of my own,
I so did paint her in her loveliness—
Pouring my heart all out upon the lines
I knew too faithfully, and lavishing
The hoarded fire of a whole age of love
Upon each passionate word, that, as I sunk
Exhausted at the close, the ravish'd crowd
Flung gold and flowers on my still quivering lyre;
And the moved monarch in his gladness swore
There was no boon beneath his kingly crown
Too high for such a minstrel!

　　　　　　　　　Did my star
Speak in my fainting ear?　Heard I the king?
Or did the audible pulses of my heart
Seem to me so articulate?　I rose,
And tore my mask away; and, as the stole
Dropp'd from my shoulders, I glanced hurriedly

A look upon the face of Lady Clare.
It was enough ! I saw that she was changed—
That a brief hour had chill'd the open child
To calculating woman—that she read
With cold displeasure my o'er-daring thought:
And on that brow, to me as legible
As stars to the rapt Arab, I could trace
The scorn that waited on me ! Sick of life,
Yet, even then, with a half-rallied hope
Prompting my faltering tongue, I blindly knelt,
And claim'd the king's fair promise—

ISIDORE.

For the hand
Of Lady Clare ?

LORD IVON.

No, sweet one—for a sword.

ISIDORE.

You surely spoke to her ?

LORD IVON.

I saw her face
No more for years. I went unto the wars;
And when again I sought that palace door,
A glory heralded the minstrel boy
That monarchs might have envied.

ISIDORE.

Was she there ?

LORD IVON.

Yes—and, O God ! how beautiful ! The last,
The ripest seal of loveliness, was set
Upon her form ; and the all-glorious pride
That I had worshipp'd on her girlish lip,

When her scared dove fled to me, was matured
Into a queenly grace; and nobleness
Was bound like a tiara to her brow,
And every motion breathed of it.   There lived
Nothing on earth so ravishingly fair.

ISIDORE.

And you still loved her?

LORD IVON.

I had perill'd life
In every shape—had battled on the sea,
And burnt upon the desert, and outgone
Spirits most mad for glory, with this one
O'ermastering hope upon me.   Honour, fame,
Gold, even, were as dust beneath my feet;
And war was my disgust, though I had sought
Its horrors like a bloodhound—for her praise.
My life was drunk up with the love of her.

ISIDORE.

And *now* she scorn'd you not?

LORD IVON.

Worse, Isidore!
She pitied me!   I did not need a voice
To tell my love.   She knew her sometime minion—
And felt that she should never be adored
With such idolatry as his, and sigh'd
That hearts so true beat not in palaces—
Bnt I was poor, with all my bright renown,
And lowly born; and she—the Lady Clare!

ISIDORE.

She could not tell you this?

LORD IVON.

                    She broke my heart
As kindly as the fisher hooks the worm—
Pitying me the while!

ISIDORE.

          And you—

LORD IVON.

                    Lived on!
But the remembrance irks me, and my throat
Chokes with the utterance!

ISIDORE.

          Dear father!

LORD IVON.

                    Nay—
Thanks to sweet Mary Mother, it is past;
And in this world I shall have no more need
To speak of it.

ISIDORE.

          But there were brighter days
In store.   My mother and this palace—

LORD IVON.

                    You outrun
My tale, dear Isidore!   But 'tis as well.
I would not linger on it.

                    Twenty years
From this heart-broken hour, I stood again,
An old man and a stranger, at the door
Of this same palace.   I had been a slave
For gold that time!   My star had wrought with me!
And I was richer than the wizard king

Throned in the mines of Ind.   I could not look
On my innumerable gems, the glare
Pain'd so my sun-struck eyes !   My gold was countless.

ISIDORE.

And Lady Clare ?

LORD IVON.

                I met upon the threshold
Her very self—all youth, all loveliness—
So like the fresh-kept picture in my brain,
That for a moment I forgot all else,
And stagger'd back and wept.   She pass'd me by
With a cold look—

ISIDORE.

            Oh ! not the Lady Clare !

LORD IVON.

Her daughter, yet herself !   But what a change
Waited me here !   My thin and grizzled locks
Were fairer now than the young minstrel's curls—
My sun-burnt visage and contracted eye
Than the gay soldier with his gallant mien !
My words were wit, my looks interpreted ;
And Lady Clare—I tell you, Lady Clare
Lean'd fondly—fondly ! on my wasted arm.
O God ! how changed my nature with all this !
I, that had been all love and tenderness—
The truest and most gentle heart, till now,
That ever beat—grew suddenly a devil !
I bought me lands, and titles, and received
Men's homage with a smooth hypocrisy ;
And—you will scarce believe me, Isidore—
I suffer'd them to wile their peerless daughter,
The image and the pride of Lady Clare,
To wed me !

ISIDORE.

Sir ! you did not !

LORD IVON.

Ay ! I saw
Th' indignant anger when her mother first
Broke the repulsive wish, and the degrees
Of shuddering reluctance as her mind
Admitted the intoxicating tales
Of wealth unlimited. And when she look'd
On my age-stricken features, and my form,
Wasted before its time, and turn'd away
To hide from me her tears, her very mother
Whisper'd the cursed comfort in her ear
That made her what she is !

ISIDORE.

You could not wed her,
Knowing all this !

LORD IVON.

I felt that I had lost
My life else. I had wrung, for forty years,
My frame to its last withers ; I had flung
My boyhood's fire away—the energy
Of a most sinless youth—the toil, and fret,
And agony of manhood. I had dared,
Fought, suffer'd, slaved—and never for an hour
Forgot or swerved from my resolve ; and now—
With the delirious draught upon my lips—
Dash down the cup !

ISIDORE.

Yet *she* had never wrong'd you !

LORD IVON.

Thou'rt pleading for thy mother, my sweet child !
And angels hear thee. But, if she was wrong'd,

The sin be on the pride that sells its blood
Coldly and only for this damning gold.
Had I not offer'd youth first?   Came I not,
With my hands brimm'd with glory, to buy love—
And was I not denied?

ISIDORE.

                        Yet, dearest father,
They forced her not to wed?

LORD IVON.

                              I call'd her back
Myself from the church threshold, and, before
Her mother and her kinsmen, bade her swear
It was her own free choice to marry me.
I show'd her my shrunk hand, and bade her think
If that was like a bridegroom, and beware
Of perjuring her chaste and spotless soul,
If now she loved me not.

ISIDORE.

                      What said she, sir?

LORD IVON.

Oh! they had made her even as themselves;
And her young heart was cooler than the slab
Unsunn'd beneath Pentelicus.   She press'd
My wither'd fingers in her dewy clasp,
And smiled up in my face, and chid "my lord"
For his wild fancies, and led on!

ISIDORE.

                            And no
Misgiving at the altar?

LORD IVON.

None! She swore
To love and cherish me till death should part us,
With a voice clear as mine.

ISIDORE.

And kept it, father!
In mercy tell me so!

LORD IVON.

She lives, my daughter!

.   .   .   .   .   .

Long ere my babe was born, my pride had ebb'd,
And let my heart down to its better founts
Of tenderness. I had no friends—not one!
My love gush'd to my wife. I rack'd my brain
To find her a new pleasure every hour—
Yet not with me—I fear'd to haunt her eye!
Only at night, when she was slumbering
In all her beauty, I would put away
The curtains till the pale night-lamp shone on her,
And watch her through my tears.

One night her lips
Parted as I gazed on them, and the name
Of a young noble, who had been my guest,
Stole forth in broken murmurs. I let fall
The curtains silently, and left her there
To slumber and dream on; and gliding forth
Upon the terrace, knelt to my pale star,
And swore, that if it pleased the God of light
To let me look upon the unborn child
Lying beneath her heart, I would but press
One kiss upon its lips, and take away
My life—that was a blight upon her years.

ISIDORE.

I was that child ?

LORD IVON.

Yes—and I heard the cry
Of thy small " piping mouth " as 'twere a call
From my remembering star. I waited only
Thy mother's strength to bear the common shock
Of death within the doors. She rose at last,
And, oh ! so sweetly pale ! And thou, my child !
My heart misgave me as I look'd upon thee ;
But he was ever at her side whose name
She murmur'd in her sleep ; and, lingering on
To drink a little of thy sweetness more
Before I died, I watch'd their stolen love
As she had been my daughter, with a pure,
Passionless joy that I should leave her soon
To love him as she would. I know not how
To tell thee more. . . .

. . . Come, sweet ! she is not worthy
Of tears like thine and mine ! . . .

. . . She fled and left me
The very night ! The poison was prepared—
And she had been a widow with the morn
Rich as Golconda. As the midnight chimed,
My star rose. Gazing on its mounting orb,
I raised the chalice—but a weakness came
Over my heart ; and, taking up the lamp,
I glided to her chamber, and removed
The curtains for a last, a parting look
Upon my child. . . .

. . . Had she but taken thee,
I could have felt she had a mother's heart,

And drain'd the chalice still.   I could not leave
My babe alone in such a heartless world!

ISIDORE.

Thank God!   Thank God!

———

THE CONFESSIONAL.

" When thou hast met with careless hearts and cold,
  Hearts that young love may touch, but never hold—
  Not changeless, as the loved and left of old—
      Remember me—remember me—
      I passionately pray of thee!"

LADY E. S. WORTLEY.

I THOUGHT of thee—I thought of thee,
    On ocean many a weary night—
When heaved the long and sullen sea,
    With only waves and stars in sight.
We stole along by isles of balm,
    We furl'd before the coming gale,
We slept amid the breathless calm,
    We flew beneath the straining sail—
But thou wert lost for years to me,
And, day and night, I thought of thee!

I thought of thee—I thought of thee,
    In France—amid the gay saloon,
Where eyes as dark as eyes may be
    Are many as the leaves in June—
Where life is love, and even the air
    Is pregnant with impassion'd thought,
And song and dance and music are
    With one warm meaning only fraught—
My half-snared heart broke lightly free,
And, with a blush, I thought of thee!

I thought of thee—I thought of thee,
　　In Florence,—where the fiery hearts
Of Italy are breathed away
　　In wonders of the deathless arts;
Where strays the Contadina down
　　Val d'Arno with a song of old;
Where clime and woman seldom frown,
　　And life runs over sands of gold;
I stray'd to lone Fiesolé
On many an eve, and thought of thee.

I thought of thee—I thought of thee,
　　In Rome,—when on the Palatine
Night left the Cæsar's palace free
　　To Time's forgetful foot and mine;
Or, on the Coliseum's wall,
　　When moonlight touch'd the ivied stone,
Reclining, with a thought of all
　　That o'er this scene has come and gone—
The shades of Rome would start and flee
Unconsciously—I thought of thee.

I thought of thee—I thought of thee,
　　In Vallombrosa's holy shade,
Where nobles born the friars be,
　　By life's rude changes humbler made.
Here Milton framed his Paradise;
　　I slept within his very cell;
And, as I closed my weary eyes,
　　I thought the cowl would fit me well—
The cloisters breathed, it seem'd to me,
Of heart's-ease—but I thought of thee.

I thought of thee—I thought of thee,
　　In Venice,—on a night in June;

When, through the city of the sea,
   Like dust of silver slept the moon.
Slow turn'd his oar the gondolier,
   And, as the black barks glided by,
The water to my leaning ear
   Bore back the lover's passing sigh—
It was no place alone to be—
I thought of thee—I thought of thee.

I thought of thee—I thought of thee,
   In the Ionian isles—when straying
With wise Ulysses by the sea—
   Old Homer's songs around me playing;
Or, watching the bewitch'd caique,
   That o'er the star-lit waters flew,
I listen'd to the helmsman Greek,
   Who sung the song that Sappho knew—
The poet's spell, the bark, the sea,
All vanish'd—as I thought of thee.

I thought of thee—I thought of thee,
   In Greece—when rose the Parthenon
Majestic o'er the Egean sea,
   And heroes with it, one by one;
When, in the grove of Academe,
   Where Lais and Leontium stray'd
Discussing Plato's mystic theme,
   I lay at noontide in the shade—
The Egean wind, the whispering tree,
Had voices—and I thought of thee.

I thought of thee—I thought of thee,
   In Asia—on the Dardanelles;
Where swiftly as the waters flee,
   Each wave some sweet old story tells;

Q

And, seated by the marble tank
  Which sleeps by Ilium's ruins old,
(The fount where peerless Helen drank,
  And Venus laved her locks of gold,)*
I thrill'd such classic haunts to see,
Yet even here—I thought of thee.

I thought of thee—I thought of thee,
  Where glide the Bosphor's lovely waters,
All palace-lined from sea to sea;
  And ever on its shores the daughters
Of the delicious East are seen,
  Printing the brink with slipper'd feet.
And oh, the snowy folds between,
  What eyes of heaven your glances meet!
Peris of light no fairer be—
Yet—in Stamboul—I thought of thee.

I've thought of thee—I've thought of thee,
  Through change that teaches to forget;
Thy face looks up from every sea,
  In every star thine eyes are set,
Though roving beneath Orient skies,
  Whose golden beauty breathes of rest,
I envy every bird that flies
  Into the far and clouded West:
I think of thee—I think of thee!
Oh, dearest! hast thou thought of me?

FLORENCE GRAY.

I was in Greece. It was the hour of noon,
And the Egean wind had dropp'd asleep

---

* In the Scamander,—before contending for the prize of beauty on
Mount Ida. Its head waters fill a beautiful tank near the walls of Troy.

Upon Hymettus, and the thymy isles
Of Salamis and Egina lay hung
Like clouds upon the bright and breathless sea.
I had climbed up the Acropolis at morn,
And hours had fled, as time will in a dream,
Amidst its deathless ruins—for the air
Is full of spirits in these mighty fanes,
And they walk with you !   As it sultrier grew,
I laid me down within a shadow deep
Of a tall column of the Parthenon,
And, in an absent idleness of thought,
I scrawl'd upon the smooth and marble base.
Tell me, O memory, what wrote I there ?
The name of a sweet child I knew at Rome !

I was in Asia.   'Twas a peerless night
Upon the plains of Sardis, and the moon,
Touching my eyelids through the wind-stirr'd tent,
Had witch'd me from my slumber.   I arose
And silently stole forth, and by the brink
Of " gold Pactolus," where his waters bathe
The bases of Cybele's columns fair,
I paced away the hours.   In wakeful mood
I mused upon the storied past awhile,
Watching the moon, that, with the same mild eye,
Had look'd upon the mighty Lydian kings
Sleeping around me—Crœsus, who had heap'd
Within that mouldering portico his gold,
And Gyges, buried with his viewless ring
Beneath yon swelling tumulus—and then
I loiter'd up the valley to a small
And humbler ruin, where the undefiled*

---

* " Thou hast a few names even in Sardis which have not defiled their garments : and they shall walk with me in white : for they are worthy." —*Revelation* iii. 4.

Of the Apocalypse their garments kept
Spotless ; and crossing with a conscious awe
The broken threshold, to my spirit's eye
It seem'd as if, amid the moonlight, stood
"The angel of the church of Sardis" still !
And I again pass'd onward, and as dawn
Paled the bright morning star, I laid me down
Weary and sad beside the river's brink,
And 'twixt the moonlight and the rosy morn,
Wrote with my finger in the "golden sands."
Tell me, O memory, what wrote I there ?
The name of a sweet child I knew at Rome !

The dust is old upon my "sandal-shoon,"
And still I am a pilgrim ; I have roved
From wild America to spicy Ind,
And worshipp'd at innumerable shrines
Of beauty ; and the painter's art, to me,
And sculpture, speak as with a living tongue,
And of dead kingdoms I recall the soul,
Sitting amid their ruins.　I have stored
My memory with thoughts that can allay
Fever and sadness, and when life gets dim,
And I am overladen in my years,
Minister to me.　But when wearily
The mind gives over toiling, and with eyes
Open but seeing not, and senses all
Lying awake within their chambers dim,
Thought settles like a fountain, still and clear—
Far in its sleeping depths, as 'twere a gem,
Tell me, O memory, what shines so fair ?
The face of the sweet child I knew at Rome !

THE PITY OF THE PARK FOUNTAIN.

'TWAS a summery day in the last of May—
   Pleasant in sun or shade ;
And the hours went by, as the poets say,
Fragrant and fair on their flowery way ;
And a hearse crept slowly through Broadway—
   And the Fountain gaily play'd.

The Fountain play'd right merrily,
   And the world look'd bright and gay ;
And a youth went by, with a restless eye,
Whose heart was sick and whose brain was dry ;
And he pray'd to God that he might die—
   And the Fountain play'd away.

Uprose the spray like a diamond throne,
   And the drops like music rang—
And of those who marvell'd how it shone,
Was a proud man, left, in his shame, alone ;
And he shut his teeth with a smother'd groan—
   And the Fountain sweetly sang.

And a rainbow spann'd it changefully,
   Like a bright ring broke in twain ;
And the pale, fair girl, who stopp'd to see,
Was sick with the pangs of poverty—
And from hunger to guilt she chose to flee
   As the rainbow smiled again.

And all as gay, on another day,
   The morning will have shone ;
And at noon, unmark'd through bright Broadway,
A hearse will take its silent way ;
And the bard who sings will have pass'd away—
   And the Fountain will play on !

" *CHAMBER SCENE.* "

[*An exquisite picture in the studio of a young artist at Rome.*]

SHE rose from her untroubled sleep,
  And put away her soft brown hair,
And, in a tone as low and deep
  As love's first whisper, breathed a prayer—
Her snow-white hands together press'd,
  Her blue eyes shelter'd in the lid,
The folded linen on her breast
  Just swelling with the charms it hid;
And from her long and flowing dress
  Escaped a bare and slender foot,
Whose shape upon the earth did press
  Like a new snow-flake, white and " mute ; "
And there, from slumber pure and warm,
  Like a young spirit fresh from heaven,
She bow'd her slight and graceful form,
  And humbly pray'd to be forgiven.

O God ! if souls unsoil'd as these
  Need daily mercy from Thy throne—
If she upon her bended knees—
  Our loveliest and our purest one—
She, with a face so clear and bright,
We deem her some stray child of light—
  If she, with those soft eyes in tears,
  Day after day in her first years,
Must kneel and pray for grace from Thee—
What far, far deeper need have we ?
  How hardly, if she win not heaven,
  Will *our* wild errors be forgiven !

THE WIFE'S APPEAL.

"Love borrows greatly from opinion. Pride, above all things, strengthens
affection."—E. L. BULWER.

HE sat and read.   A book with silver clasps,
All gorgeous with illuminated lines
Of gold and crimson, lay upon a frame
Before him.   'Twas a volume of old time;
And in it were fine mysteries of the stars
Solved with a cunning wisdom, and strange thoughts,
Half prophecy, half poetry, and dreams
Clearer than truth, and speculations wild
That touch'd the secrets of your very soul,
They were so based on Nature.   With a face
Glowing with thought, he pored upon the book.
The cushions of an Indian loom lay soft
Beneath his limbs, and, as he turn'd the page,
The sunlight, streaming through the curtain's fold,
Fell from the rose-tint on his jewell'd hand;
And the rich woods of the quaint furniture
Lay deepening their vein'd colours in the sun,
And the stain'd marbles on the pedestals
Stood like a silent company—Voltaire,
With an infernal sneer upon his lips;
And Socrates, with godlike human love
Stamp'd on his countenance; and orators,
Of times gone by that made them; and old bards,
And Medicean Venus, half divine.
Around the room were shelves of dainty lore,
And rich old pictures hung upon the walls
Where the slant light fell on them; and wrought gems,
Medallions, rare mosaics, and antiques
From Herculaneum, the niches fill'd;
And on the table of enamel, wrought

With a lost art in Italy, there lay
Prints of fair women, and engravings rare,
And a new poem, and a costly toy;
And in their midst a massive lamp of bronze
Burning sweet spices constantly. Asleep
Upon the carpet couch'd a graceful hound,
Of a rare breed; and, as his master gave
A murmur of delight at some sweet line,
He raised his slender head, and kept his eye
Upon him till the pleasant smile had pass'd
From his mild lips, and then he slept again.
The light beyond the crimson folds grew dusk,
And the clear letters of the pleasant book
Mingled and blurr'd, and the lithe hound rose up,
And, with his earnest eye upon the door,
Listen'd attentively. It came as wont—
The fall of a light foot upon the stair—
And the fond animal sprang out to meet
His mistress, and caress the ungloved hand,
He seem'd to know was beautiful. She stoop'd
Gracefully down and touch'd his silken ears
As she pass'd in—then, with a tenderness,
Half playful and half serious, she knelt
Upon the ottoman and press'd her lips
Upon her husband's forehead.

.   .   .   .   .

She rose and put the curtain-folds aside
From the high window, and look'd out upon
The shining stars in silence. "Look they not
Like Paradises to thine eye?" he said—
But, as he spoke, a tear fell through the light—
And—starting from his seat—he folded her
Close to his heart, and—with unsteady voice—
Ask'd—if she was not happy. A faint smile
Broke through her tears; and pushing off the hair

From his broad forehead, she held back his head
With her white hand, and, gazing on his face,
Gave to her heart free utterance :—

"Happy ?—yes, dearest !—blest
Beyond the limit of my wildest dream—
Too bright, indeed, my blessings ever seem ;
There lives not in my breast
One of Hope's promises by Love unkept,
And yet—forgive me, Ernest—I have wept.

"How shall I speak of sadness,
And seem not thankless to my God and thee ?
How can the lightest wish but seem to be
The very whim of madness ?
Yet, oh, there is a boon thy love beside—
And I will ask it of thee—in my pride !

"List, while my boldness lingers !
If thou hadst won yon twinkling star to hear thee—
If thou couldst bid the rainbow's curve bend near thee—
If thou couldst charm thy fingers
To weave for thee the sunset's tent of gold—
Wouldst in thine own heart treasure it untold ?

"If thou hadst Ariel's gift,
To course the veined metals of the earth—
If thou couldst wind a fountain to its birth—
If thou couldst know the drift
Of the lost cloud that sail'd into the sky—
Wouldst keep it for thine own unanswer'd eye ?

"It is thy life and mine !—
Thou, in thyself—and I in thee—misprison
Gifts like a circle of bright stars unrisen—
For thou whose mind should shine,

Eminent as a planet's light, art here—
Moved with the starting of a woman's tear.

    " I have told o'er thy powers
In secret, as a miser tells his gold ;
I know thy spirit calm, and true, and bold :
    I've watch'd thy lightest hours,
And seen thee, in the wildest flush of youth,
Touch'd with the instinct ravishment of truth.

    " Thou hast the secret strange
To read that hidden book, the human heart ;
Thou hast the ready writer's practised art ;
    Thou hast the thought to range
The broadest circles Intellect hath ran—
And thou art God's best work—an honest man.

    " And yet thou slumberest here
Like a caged bird that never knew its pinions,
And others track in glory the dominions
    Where thou hast not thy peer—
Setting their weaker eyes unto the sun,
And plucking honour that thou shouldst have won.

    " Oh, if thou lovedst me ever,
Ernest, my husband !—if th' idolatry
That lets go heaven to fling its all on thee—
    If to dismiss thee never
In dream or prayer, have given me aught to claim—
Heed me—oh, heed me ! and awake to fame ! "

                      Her lips
Closed with an earnest sweetness, and she sat
Gazing into his eyes as if her look
Search'd their dark orbs for answer.   The hot blood
Into his temples mounted, and across
His countenance the flush of passionate thoughts

Pass'd with irresolute quickness.   He rose up
And paced the dim room rapidly awhile,
Calming his troubled mind; and then he came
And laid his hand upon her orbéd brow,
And in a voice of heavenly tenderness
Answer'd her :—

   " Before I knew thee, Mary,
Ambition was my angel.   I did hear
For ever its witch'd voices in mine ear ;
   My days were visionary—
My nights were like the slumbers of the mad—
And every dream swept o'er me glory-clad.

   " I read the burning letters
Of warlike pomp, on History's page, alone ;
I counted nothing the struck widow's moan ;
   I heard no clank of fetters ;
I only felt the trumpet's stirring blast,
And lean-eyed Famine stalk'd unchallenged past !

   " I heard with veins of lightning
The utterance of the Statesman's word of power—
Binding and loosing nations in an hour—
   But, while my eye was bright'ning,
A mask'd detraction breathed upon his fame,
And a cursed serpent slimed his written name.

   " The Poet rapt mine ears
With the transporting music that he sung.
With fibres from his life his lyre he strung,
   And bathed the world in tears—
And then he turn'd away to muse apart,
And Scorn stole after him—and broke his heart !

   " Yet here and there I saw
One who did set the world at calm defiance,

And press right onward with a bold reliance;
   And he did seem to awe
The very shadows pressing on his breast,
And, with a strong heart, held himself at rest.

   " And then I look'd again—
And he had shut the door upon the crowd,
And on his face he lay and groan'd aloud—
   Wrestling with hidden pain;
And in her chamber sat his wife in tears,
And his sweet babes grew sad with whisper'd fears.

   " And so I turn'd sick-hearted
From the bright cup away, and, in my sadness,
Search'd mine own bosom for some spring of gladness;
   And lo! a fountain started
Whose waters even in death flow calm and fast,
And my wild fever-thirst was slaked at last.

   " And then I met thee, Mary,
And felt how love may into fulness pour,
Like light into a fountain running o'er:
   And I did hope to vary
My life but with surprises sweet as this—
A dream—but for thy waking—fill'd with bliss.

   " Yet now I feel my spirit
Bitterly stirr'd, and—nay, lift up thy brow!
It is thine own voice echoing to thee now,
   And thou didst pray to hear it—
I must unto my work and my stern hours!
Take from my room thy harp, and books, and flowers!

.   .   .   .

.   .   .   .   .   . A year—
And in his room again he sat alone.
His frame had lost its fulness in that time;
His manly features had grown sharp and thin,

And from his lips the constant smile had faded.
Wild fires had burn'd the languor from his eye :
The lids look'd fever'd, and the brow was bent
With an habitual frown. He was much changed.
His chin was resting on his clenchéd hand,
And with his foot he beat upon the floor,
Unconsciously, the time of a sad tune.
Thoughts of the past prey'd on him bitterly.
He had won power and held it. He had walk'd
Steadily upward to the eye of Fame,
And kept his truth unsullied—but his home
Had been invaded by envenom'd tongues ;
His wife—his spotless wife—had been assail'd
By slander, and his child had grown afraid
To come to him—his manner was so stern.
He could not speak beside his own hearth freely.
His friends were half estranged, and vulgar men
Presumed upon their services and grew
Familiar with him. He'd small time to sleep,
And none to pray ; and, with his heart in fetters,
He bore harsh insults silently, and bow'd
Respectfully to men who knew he loathed them !
And, when his heart was eloquent with truth,
And love of country, and an honest zeal
Burn'd for expression, he could find no words
They would not misinterpret with their lies.
What were his many honours to him now ?
The good half doubted, falsehood was so strong—
His home was hateful with its cautious fears—
His wife lay trembling on his very breast
Frighted with calumny !—And this is FAME !

TO A STOLEN RING.

Oh for thy history now!   Hadst thou a tongue
To whisper of thy secrets, I could lay
Upon thy jewell'd tracery mine ear,
And dream myself in heaven.   Thou hast been worn
In that fair creature's pride, and thou hast felt
The bounding of the haughtiest blood that e'er
Sprang from the heart of woman; and thy gold
Has lain upon her forehead in the hour
Of sadness, when the weary thoughts came fast,
And life was but a bitterness with all
Its vividness and beauty.   She has gazed
In her fair girlhood on thy snowy pearls,
And mused away the hours, and she has bent
On thee the downcast radiance of her eye
When a deep tone was eloquent in her ear,
And thou hast lain upon her cheek, and press'd
Back on her heart its beatings, and put by
From her vein'd temples the luxuriant curls;
And in her peaceful sleep, when she has lain
In her unconscious beauty, and the dreams
Of her high heart came goldenly and soft,
Thou hast been there unchidden, and hast felt
The swelling of the clear transparent veins
As the rich blood rush'd through them, warm and fast.
I am impatient as I gaze on thee,
Thou inarticulate jewel!   Thou hast heard
With thy dull ear such music!—the low tone
Of a young sister's tenderness, when night
Has folded them together like one flower—
The sudden snatch of a remember'd song
Warbled capriciously—the careless word
Lightly betraying the inaudible thought

Working within the heart ; and more, than all,
Thou hast been lifted when the fervent prayer
For a loved mother, or the sleeping one
Lying beside her, trembling on her lip,
And the warm tear that from her eye stole out
As the soft lash fell over it, has lain
Amid thy shining jewels like a star.

TO HER WHO HAS HOPES OF ME.

OH stern, yet lovely monitress !
  Thine eye should be of colder hue,
And on thy neck a paler tress
  Should toy among those veins of blue !
  For thou art to thy mission true—
An angel clad in human guise—
But sinners sometimes have such eyes,
  And braid for love such tresses too ;
And, while thou talk'st to me of heaven,
I sigh that thou hast not a sin to be forgiven !

Night comes, with love upon the breeze,
  And the calm clock strikes, stilly, " ten."
  I start to hear it beat, for then
I know that thou art on thy knees—
  And, at that hour, where'er thou be,
  Ascends to heaven a prayer for me !
  My heart drops to its bended knee—
The mirth upon my lip is dumb—
Yet, as a thought of heaven would come,
  There glides, before it, one of thee—
Thou, in thy white dress, kneeling there !—
I fear I could leave heaven to see thee at thy prayer !

I follow up the sacred aisle,
  Thy light step on the Sabbath-day,
And—as perhaps thou pray'st the while—
  My light thoughts pass away !
As swells in air the holy hymn,
My breath comes thick, my eyes are dim,
  And through my tears I pray !
I do not think my heart is stone—
But, while for heaven it beats alone—
  In heaven would willing stay—
One rustle of thy snow-white gown
  Sends all my thoughts astray !
The preaching dies upon my ear—
What is " the better world " when thy dark eyes are here ?

Yet pray ! my years have been but few—
  And many a wile the tempter weaves,
  And many a saint the sinner grieves
    Ere Mercy brings him through !
But oh, when Mercy sits serene
    And strives to bend to me,
Pray, that the cloud which comes between
    May less resemble thee !
The world that would my soul beguile
Tints all its roses with thy smile !
    In heaven 'twere well to be !
But,—to desire that blessed shore—
O lady ! thy dark eyes must first have gone before !

"*SHE WAS NOT THERE.*"

"The bird,
Let loose, to his far nest will flee,
  And love, though breathed but on a word,
Will find thee, over land and sea."

'Tis midnight deep—I came but now
  From the close air of lighted halls ;
And while I hold my aching brow
  I gaze upon my dim-lit walls ;
And, feeling here that I am free
  To wear the look that suits my mood,
And let my thoughts flow back to thee,
  I bless my tranquil solitude,
And bidding all thoughts else begone,
I muse upon thy love alone.
Yet was the music sweet to-night,
  And fragrant odours fill'd the air,
And flowers were drooping in the light,
  And lovely women wander'd there ;
And fruits and wines with lavish waste
  Were on the marble tables piled,
And all that tempts the eye and taste,
  And sets the haggard pulses wild,
And wins from care, and deadens sadness,
Were there—but yet I felt no gladness.
I thought of thee—I thought of thee—
  Each cunning change the music play'd,
Each fragrant breath that stole to me,
  My wandering thought more truant made.
The lovely women pass'd me by,
  The wit fell powerless on mine ear,
I look'd on all with vacant eye,
  I did not see—I did not hear !

The skill'd musician's master-tone
    Was sweet—thy voice were sweeter far!
They were soft eyes the lamps shone on—
    The eyes I worship gentler are!
The halls were broad, the mirrors tall,
    With silver lamps and costly wine—
I only thought how poor was all
    To one low tone from lips like thine—
I only felt how well forgot
Were all the stars look on—*and thy sweet eyes do not!*

FAIL ME NOT THOU!

> "Oh, by that little word
> How many thoughts are stirr'd!—
> The last, the last, the last!"

THE star may but a meteor be,
    That breaks upon the stormy night;
And I may err, believing thee
    A spark of heaven's own changeless light!
But if on earth beams aught so fair,
    It seems, of all the lights that shine,
Serenest in its truth, 'tis there,
    Burning in those soft eyes of thine.
Yet long-watch'd stars from heaven have rush'd,
    And long-loved friends have dropp'd away,
And mine—my very heart have crush'd!
    And I have hoped this many a day,
It lived no more for love or pain!
But thou hast stirr'd its depths again,
    And, to its dull, out-wearied ear,
Thy voice of melody has crept,
    In tones it cannot choose but hear;
And now I feel it only slept,

And know, at even thy lightest smile,
  It gather'd fire and strength the while.
Fail me not thou !   This feeling past,
  My heart would never rouse again.
Thou art the brightest—but the last !
  And if *this* trust, *this* love is vain—
If thou, all peerless as thou art,
Be not less fair than true of heart—
  My loves are o'er !   The sun will shine
Upon no grave so hush'd as this dark breast of mine.

TO M——, FROM ABROAD.

> "The desire of the moth for the star—
>   Of the night for the morrow—
> The devotion to something afar
>   From the sphere of our sorrow."
> —Shelley.

> "L'alma, quel che non ha, sogna e figura."
> —Metastasio.

As, gazing on the Pleiades,
  We count each fair and starry one,
Yet wander from the light of these
  To muse upon the Pleiad gone—
As, bending o'er fresh-gather'd flowers,
  The rose's most enchanting hue
Reminds us but of other hours
  Whose roses were all lovely too—
So, dearest, when I rove among
  The bright ones of this foreign sky,
And mark the smile, and list the song,
  And watch the dancers gliding by,
The fairer still they seem to be,
The more it stirs a thought of thee !

The sad, sweet bells of twilight chime,
  Of many hearts may touch but one,
And so this seeming careless rhyme
  Will whisper to thy heart alone.
I give it to the winds!   The bird,
  Let loose, to his far nest will flee,
And love, though breathed but on a word,
  Will find thee over land and sea.
Though clouds across the sky have driven,
  We trust the star at last will shine,
And like the very light of heaven
  I trust thy love.   *Trust thou in mine!*

TO A FACE BELOVED.

THE music of the waken'd lyre
  Dies not upon the quivering strings,
Nor burns alone the minstrel's fire
  Upon the lip that trembling sings;
Nor shines the moon in heaven unseen,
  Nor shuts the flower its fragrant cells,
Nor sleeps the fountain's wealth, I ween,
  For ever in its sparry wells—
The spells of the enchanter lie
Not on his own lone heart—his own rapt ear and eye.

I look upon a face as fair
  As ever made a lip of heaven
Falter amid its music-prayer!
  The first-lit star of summer even
Springs not so softly on the eye,
  Nor grows, with watching, half so bright,
Nor 'mid its sisters of the sky,
  So seems of heaven the dearest light—

Men murmur, where that face is seen,
My youth's angelic dream was of that look and mien.

Yet though we deem the stars are blest,
    And envy, in our grief, the flower
That bears but sweetness in its breast,
    And fear th' enchanter for his power,
And love the minstrel for the spell
    He winds out of his lyre so well—
The stars are almoners of light,
    The lyrist of melodious air,
The fountain of its waters bright,
    And everything most sweet and fair
Of that by which it charms the ear,
    The eye, of him that passes near—
A lamp is lit in woman's eye
That souls, else lost on earth, remember angels by.

———

BETTER MOMENTS.

My mother's voice! how often creeps
    Its cadence on my lonely hours!
Like healing sent on wings of sleep,
    Or dew to the unconscious flowers.

I can forget her melting prayer
    While leaping pulses madly fly,
But in the still, unbroken air,
    Her gentle tone comes stealing by—
And years, and sin, and manhood flee,
And leave me at my mother's knee.

The book of nature, and the print
    Of beauty on the whispering sea,

Give aye to me some lineament
   Of what I have been taught to be,
My heart is harder, and perhaps
   My manliness hath drunk up tears;
And there's a mildew in the lapse
   Of a few swift and chequer'd years—
But nature's book is even yet
With all my mother's lessons writ.

I have been out at eventide
   Beneath a moonlight sky of spring,
When earth was garnish'd like a bride,
   And night had on her silver wing—
When bursting leaves, and diamond grass,
   And waters leaping to the light,
And all that make the pulses pass
   With wilder fleetness, throng'd the night—
When all was beauty—then have I
   With friends on whom my love is flung
Like myrrh on winds of Araby,
   Gazed up where evening's lamp is hung,
And when the beautiful spirit there
   Flung over me its golden chain,
My mother's voice came on the air
   Like the light dropping of the rain—
And resting on some silver star
   The spirit of a bended knee,
I've pour'd out low and fervent prayer
   That our eternity might be
To rise in heaven, like stars at night
To tread a living path of light.

I have been on the dewy hills,
   When night was stealing from the dawn,
And mist was on the waking rills,
   And tints were delicately drawn

In the grey East—when birds were waking,
  With a low murmur in the trees,
And melody by fits was breaking
  Upon the whisper of the breeze—
And this when I was forth, perchance
As a worn reveller from the dance—
  And when the sun sprang gloriously
And freely up, and hill and river
  Were catching upon wave and tree
The arrows from his subtle quiver—
  I say a voice has thrill'd me then,
Heard on the still and rushing light,
  Or, creeping from the silent glen,
Like words from the departing night,
  Hath stricken me, and I have press'd
On the wet grass my fever'd brow,
  And pouring forth the earliest
First prayer, with which I learn'd to bow,
  Have felt my mother's spirit rush
Upon me as in by-past years,
  And, yielding to the blessed gush
Of my ungovernable tears,
  Have risen up—the gay, the wild—
  Subdued and humble as a child.

SUNRISE THOUGHTS AT THE CLOSE OF A BALL.

Morn in the East ! How coldly fair
  It breaks upon my fever'd eye !
How chides the calm and dewy air !
  How chides the pure and pearly sky !
The stars melt in a brighter fire—
  The dew, in sunshine, leaves the flowers—

They, from their watch, in light retire,
  While we, in sadness, pass from ours.

I turn from the rebuking morn,—
  The cold grey sky, and fading star,—
And listen to the harp and horn,
  And see the waltzers near and far—
The lamps and flowers are bright as yet,
  And lips beneath more bright than they,—
How can a scene so fair beget
  The mournful thoughts we bear away!

'Tis something that thou art not here,
  Sweet lover of my lightest word!
'Tis something that my mother's tear
  By these forgetful hours is stirr'd!
But I have long a loiterer been
  In haunts where Joy is said to be,
And though with Peace I enter in,
  The nymph comes never forth with me!

———

UNSEEN SPIRITS.

THE shadows lay along Broadway,
  'Twas near the twilight-tide—
And slowly there a lady fair
  Was walking in her pride.
Alone walk'd she; but, viewlessly,
  Walk'd spirits at her side.

Peace charm'd the street beneath her feet,
  And Honour charm'd the air;
And all astir look'd kind on her,
  And call'd her good as fair—

For all God ever gave to her
    She kept with chary care.

She kept with care her beauties rare
    From lovers warm and true—
For her heart was cold to all but gold,
    And the rich came not to woo—
But honour'd well are charms to sell,
    If priests the selling do.

Now walking there was one more fair—
    A slight girl, lily-pale;
And she had unseen company
    To make the spirit quail—
'Twixt Want and Scorn she walk'd forlorn,
    And nothing could avail.

No mercy now can clear her brow
    For this world's peace to pray;
For, as love's wild prayer dissolved in air,
    Her woman's heart gave way!—
But the sin forgiven by Christ in heaven
    By man is cursed alway!

THE ANNOYER.

"Common as light is love,
And its familiar voice wearies not ever."—SHELLEY.

LOVE knowest every form of air,
    And every shape of earth,
And comes, unbidden, everywhere,
    Like thought's mysterious birth.
The moonlit sea and the sunset sky
    Are written with Love's words,

And you hear his voice unceasingly,
　　Like song in the time of birds.

He peeps into the warrior's heart
　　From the tip of a stooping plume,
And the serried spears and the many men
　　May not deny him room.
He'll come to his tent in the weary night,
　　And be busy in his dream ;
And he'll float to his eye in morning light
　　Like a fay on a silver beam.

He hears the sound of the hunter's gun,
　　And rides on the echo back,
And sighs in his ear, like a stirring leaf,
　　And flits in his woodland track.
The shade of the wood, and the sheen of the river,
　　The cloud and the open sky—
He will haunt them all with his subtle quiver,
　　Like the light of your very eye.

The fisher hangs over the leaning boat,
　　And ponders the silver sea,
For Love is under the surface hid,
　　And a spell of thought has he.
He heaves the wave like a bosom sweet,
　　And speaks in the ripple low,
Till the bait is gone from the crafty line,
　　And the hook hangs bare below.

He blurs the print of the scholar's book,
　　And intrudes in the maiden's prayer,
And profanes the cell of the holy man,
　　In the shape of a lady fair.

In the darkest night, and the bright daylight,
   In earth, and sea, and sky,
In every home of human thought,
   Will Love be lurking nigh.

THE TORN HAT.

> "... A leaf
> Fresh flung upon a river, that will dance
> Upon the wave that stealeth out its life,
> Then sink of its own heaviness."
> —PHILIP SLINGSBY.

THERE'S something in a noble boy,
   A brave, free-hearted, careless one,
With his uncheck'd, unbidden joy,
   His dread of books and love of fun,
And in his clear and ready smile,
Unshaded by a thought of guile,
   And unrepress'd by sadness—
Which brings me to my childhood back,
As if I trod its very track,
   And felt its very gladness.
And yet it is not in his play,
   When every trace of thought is lost,
And not when you would call him gay,
   That his bright presence thrills me most.
His shout may ring upon the hill,
His voice be echoed in the hall,
   His merry laugh like music trill,
And I unheeding hear it all—
   For, like the wrinkles on my brow,
   I scarcely notice such things now—
But when, amid the earnest game
   He stops, as if he music heard,

And, heedless of his shouted name
As of the carol of a bird,
Stands gazing on the empty air
As if some dream were passing there—
'Tis then that on his face I look,
His beautiful but thoughtful face,
And, like a long-forgotten book,
Its sweet, familiar meanings trace—
Remembering a thousand things
Which pass'd me on those golden wings,
Which time has fetter'd now—
Things that came o'er me with a thrill,
And left me silent, sad, and still,
And threw upon my brow
A holier and a gentler cast,
That was too innocent to last.

'Tis strange how thought upon a child
Will, like a presence, sometimes press—
And when his pulse is beating wild,
And life itself is in excess—
When foot and hand, and ear and eye,
Are all with ardour straining high—
How in his heart will spring
A feeling, whose mysterious thrall
Is stronger, sweeter far than all;
And, on its silent wing,
How with the clouds he'll float away,
As wandering and as lost as they!

DAWN.

"*That* line I learned not in the old sad song."—CHARLES LAMB.

THROW up the window! 'Tis a morn for life
In its most subtle luxury.   The air
Is like a breathing from a rarer world ;
And the south wind is like a gentle friend,
Parting the hair so softly on my brow.
It has come over gardens, and the flowers
That kiss'd it are betray'd ; for as it parts,
With its invisible fingers, my loose hair,
I know it has been trifling with the rose,
And stooping to the violet.   There is joy
For all God's creatures in it.   The wet leaves
Are stirring at its touch, and birds are singing
As if to breathe were music ; and the grass
Sends up its modest odour with the dew,
Like the small tribute of humility.

I had awoke from an unpleasant dream,
And light was welcome to me.   I look'd out
To feel the common air, and when the breath
Of the delicious morning met my brow,
Cooling its fever, and the pleasant sun
Shone on familiar objects, it was like
The feeling of the captive who comes forth
From darkness to the cheerful light of day.
Oh! could we wake from sorrow ; were it all
A troubled dream like this, to cast aside
Like an untimely garment with the morn ;
Could the long fever of the heart be cool'd
By a sweet breath from nature ; or the gloom
Of a bereaved affection pass away

With looking on the lively tint of flowers—
How lightly were the spirit reconciled
To make this beautiful, bright world its home!

———

TO LAURA W——, TWO YEARS OF AGE.

BRIGHT be the skies that cover thee,
　　Child of the sunny brow—
Bright as the dream flung over thee—
　　By all that meets thee now—
Thy heart is beating joyously,
　　Thy voice is like a bird's—
And sweetly breaks the melody
　　Of thy imperfect words.
I know no fount that gushes out
　　As gladly as thy tiny shout.

I would that thou might'st ever be
　　As beautiful as now,—
That time might ever leave as free
　　Thy yet unwritten brow:
I would life were "all poetry"
　　To gentle measure set,
That nought but chasten'd melody
　　Might stain thine eye of jet—
Nor one discordant note be spoken,
Till God the cunning harp hath broken.

I would—but deeper things than these
　　With woman's lot are wove;
Wrought of intensest sympathies,
　　And nerved by purest love—
By the strong spirit's discipline,
　　By the fierce wrong forgiven,

By all that wrings the heart of sin,
  Is woman won to heaven.
"Her lot is on thee," lovely child—
God keep thy spirit undefiled!

I fear thy gentle loveliness,
  Thy witching tone and air,
Thine eye's beseeching earnestness
  May be to thee a snare.
The silver stars may purely shine,
  The waters taintless flow—
But they who kneel at woman's shrine,
  Breathe on it as they bow—
Peace may fling back the gift again,
But the crush'd flower will leave a stain.

What shall preserve thee, beautiful child?
  Keep thee as thou art now?
Bring thee, a spirit undefiled,
  At God's pure throne to bow?
The world is but a broken reed,
  And life grows early dim—
Who shall be near thee in thy need,
  To lead thee up to Him?
He, who Himself was "undefiled"?
With him we trust thee, beautiful child!

SONNET.

Storm had been on the hills.   The day had worn
  As if a sleep upon the hours had crept;
And the dark clouds that gather'd at the morn
  In dull, impenetrable masses slept,

And the wet leaves hung droopingly, and all
Was like the mournful aspect of a pall.

   Suddenly, on the horizon's edge, a blue
And delicate line, as of a pencil, lay,
   And, as it wider and intenser grew,
The darkness removed silently away,
   And, with the splendour of a God, broke through
The perfect glory of departing day:
   So, when his stormy pilgrimage is o'er,
   Will light upon the dying Christian pour.

THE SOLDIER'S WIDOW.

[*Written for a Picture.*]

   WOE for mine vine-clad home!
That it should ever be so dark to me,
With its bright threshold, and its whispering tree!
   That I should ever come,
Fearing the lonely echo of a tread
Beneath the roof-tree of my glorious dead!

   Lead on, my orphan boy!
Thy home is not so desolate to thee—
And the low shiver in the linden tree
   May bring to thee a joy;
But oh, how dark is the bright home before thee,
To her who with a joyous spirit bore thee!

   Lead on! for thou art now
My sole remaining helper.   God hath spoken,
And the strong heart I lean'd upon is broken;
   And I have seen his brow—
The forehead of my upright one, and just—
Trod by the hoof of battle in the dust.

He will not meet thee there
Who blest thee at the eventide, my son !
And when the shadows of the night steal on,
He will not call to prayer.
The lips that melted, giving thee to God,
Are in the icy keeping of the sod !

Ay, my own boy ! thy sire
Is with the sleepers of the valley cast,
And the proud glory of my life hath pass'd
With his high glance of fire.
Woe that the linden and the vine should bloom,
And a just man be gather'd to the tomb !

Why—bear them proudly, boy !
It is the sword he girded to his thigh—
It is the helm he wore in victory—
And shall we have no joy ?
For thy green vales, O Switzerland, he died—
I will forget my sorrow in my pride !

———

ON THE DEATH OF A YOUNG GIRL.

'TIS difficult to feel that she is dead.
Her presence, like the shadow of a wing
That is just lessening in the upper sky,
Lingers upon us.   We can hear her voice,
And for her step we listen, and the eye
Looks for her wonted coming with a strange,
Forgetful earnestness.   We cannot feel
That she will no more come—that from her cheek
The delicate flush has faded, and the light
Dead in her soft dark eye, and on her lip,
That was so exquisitely pure, the dew
Of the damp grave has fallen !   Who so loved,

s

Is left among the living ?   Who has walk'd
The world with such a winning loveliness,
And on its bright brief journey gather'd up
Such treasures of affection ?   She was loved
Only as idols are.   She was the pride
Of her familiar sphere—the daily joy
Of all who on her gracefulness might gaze,
And in the light and music of her way,
Have a companion's portion.   Who could feel,
While looking upon beauty such as hers,
That it would ever perish ?   It is like
The melting of a star into the sky
While you are gazing on it, or a dream
In its most ravishing sweetness rudely broken.

STARLIGHT.

THE evening star will twinkle presently.
The last small bird is silent, and the bee
Has gone into his hive, and the shut flowers
Are bending as if sleeping on the stem,
And all sweet living things are slumbering
In the deep hush of nature's resting time.
The faded West looks deep, as if its blue
Were searchable, and even as I look,
The twilight hath stole over it, and made
Its liquid eye apparent, and above
To the far-stretching zenith, and around,
As if they waited on her like a queen,
Have stole out the innumerable stars
To twinkle like intelligence in heaven.
Is it not beautiful, my fair Adel !
Fit for the young affections to come out
And bathe in like an element !   How well

The night is made for tenderness—so still
That the low whisper, scarcely audible,
Is heard like music, and so deeply pure
That the fond thought is chasten'd as it springs
And on the lip made holy.   I have won
Thy heart, my gentle girl! but it hath been
When that soft eye was on me, and the love
I told beneath the evening influence
Shall be as constant as its gentle star.

ACROSTIC-SONNET.

ELEGANCE floats about thee like a dress,
   Melting the airy motion of thy form
Into one swaying grace; and loveliness,
   Like a rich tint that makes a picture warm,
Is lurking in the chestnut of thy tress,
   Enriching it, as moonlight after storm
Mingles dark shadows into gentleness.
   A beauty that bewilders like a spell
Reigns in thine eye's clear hazel, and thy brow,
   So pure in vein'd transparency, doth tell
How spiritually beautiful art thou—
   A temple where angelic love might dwell.
Life in thy presence were a thing to keep,
Like a gay dreamer clinging to his sleep.

MAY.

OH, the merry May has pleasant hours,
   And dreamily they glide,
As if they floated like the leaves
   Upon a silver tide.

The trees are full of crimson buds,
   And the woods are full of birds,
And the waters flow to music,
   Like a tune with pleasant words.

The verdure of the meadow-land
   Is creeping to the hills,
The sweet, blue-bosom'd violets
   Are blowing by the rills;
The lilac has a load of balm
   For every wind that stirs,
And the larch stands green and beautiful
   Amid the sombre firs.

There's perfume upon every wind—
   Music in every tree—
Dews for the moisture-loving flowers—
   Sweets for the sucking bee;
The sick come forth for the healing South,
   The young are gathering flowers;
And life is a tale of poetry,
   That is told by golden hours.

If 'tis not a true philosophy,
   That the spirit when set free
Still lingers about its olden home,
   In the flower and the tree,
It is very strange that our pulses thrill
   At the sight of a voiceless thing,
And our hearts yearn so with tenderness
   In the beautiful time of Spring.

————

ROARING BROOK.

[*A passage of scenery in Connecticut.*]

It was a mountain stream that with the leap
Of its impatient waters had worn out
A channel in the rock, and wash'd away
The earth that had upheld the tall old trees,
Till it was darken'd with the shadowy arch
Of the o'er-leaning branches.   Here and there
It loiter'd in a broad and limpid pool
That circled round demurely, and anon
Sprung violently over where the rock
Fell suddenly, and bore its bubbles on,
Till they were broken by the hanging moss,
As anger with a gentle word grows calm.
In spring-time, when the snows were coming down,
And in the flooding of the autumn rains,
No foot might enter there—but in the hot
And thirsty summer, when the fountains slept
You could go up its channel in the shade,
To the far sources, with a brow as cool
As in the grotto of the anchorite.
Here when an idle student have I come,
And in a hollow of the rock lain down
And mused until the eventide, or read
Some fine old poet till my nook became
A haunt of faery, or the busy flow
Of water to my spell-bewilder'd ear
Seem'd like the din of some gay tournament.
Pleasant have been such hours, and though the wise
Have said that I was indolent, and they
Who taught me have reproved me that I play'd
The truant in the leafy month of June,

I deem it true philosophy in him
Whose path is in the rude and busy world,
To loiter with these wayside comforters.

———

THE SOLITARY.

ALONE ! alone !   How drear it is
   Always to be alone !
In such a depth of wilderness,
   The only thinking one !
The waters in their path rejoice,
   The trees together sleep—
But I have not one silver voice
   Upon my ear to creep !

The sun upon the silent hills
   His mesh of beauty weaves,
There's music in the laughing rills
   And in the whispering leaves.
The red deer like the breezes fly
   To meet the bounding roe,
But I have not a human sigh
   To cheer me as I go.

I've hated men—I hate them now—
   But, since they are not here,
I thirst for the familiar brow—
   Thirst for the stealing tear.
And I should love to see the one,
   And feel the other creep,
And then again I'd be alone
   Amid the forest deep.

I thought that I should love my hound—
   Hear my resounding gun,

Till I forgot the thrilling sound
   Of voices—one by one.
I thought that in the leafy hush
   Of nature they would die;
But, as the hinder'd waters rush,
   Resisted feelings fly.

I'm weary of my lonely hut
   And of its blasted tree,
The very lake is like my lot,
   So silent constantly.
I've lived amid the forest gloom
   Until I almost fear—
When will the thrilling voices come
   My spirit thirsts to hear?

———

AN APOLOGY

For avoiding, after long separation, a woman once loved.

SEE me no more on earth, I pray;
   Thy picture, in my memory now,
Is fair as morn, and fresh as May!
   Few were as beautiful as thou!
And still I see that willowy form—
   And still that cheek like roses dyed—
And still that dark eye, deep and warm—
   Thy look of love—thy step of pride!—
Thy memory is a star to me,
   More bright as day-beams fade and flee.

But thou, indeed!—Ah! years have fled,
   And thou, like others, changed the while—
For joy upon the lip lies dead
   If pain but cloud the sunny smile!

And care will make the roses pale,
　　And tears will soil the lily's whiteness,
And ere life's lamp begins to fail
　　The eye forgets its trick of brightness !
Look for the rose of dawn at noon,
And weep for beauty lost as soon !

Cold words that hide the envious thought !
　　I could not bear thy face to see—
But oh, 'tis not that time has wrought
　　A change in features dear to me !
No ! had it been my lot to share
　　The fragrance of the flower decay'd—
If I had borne but half the care
　　That on thy brow its burden laid—
If in *my* love thou'dst burn'd away,
The ashes still had warm'd the heart so cold to-day !

———

TO HELEN IN A HUFF.

NAY, lady, one frown is enough
　　In a life as soon over as this—
And though minutes seem long in a huff,
　　They're minutes 'tis pity to miss !
The smiles you imprison so lightly
　　Are reckon'd, like days in eclipse ;
And though you may smile again brightly,
　　You've lost so much light from your lips !
　　　　Pray, lady, smile !

The cup that is longest untasted
　　May be with our bliss running o'er,
And, love when we will, we have wasted
　　An age in not loving before !

Perchance Cupid's forging a fetter
To tie us together some day,
And, just for the chance, we had better
Be laying up love, I should say !
Nay, lady, smile !

ON THE DEATH OF EDWARD PAYSON, D.D.

A SERVANT of the living God is dead !
His errand hath been well and early done,
And early hath he gone to his reward.
He shall come no more forth, but to his sleep
Hath silently lain down, and so shall rest.

Would ye bewail our brother ?   He hath gone
To Abraham's bosom.   He shall no more thirst,
Nor hunger, but for ever in the eye
Holy and meek, of Jesus, he may look,
Unchided, and untempted, and unstain'd.
Would ye bewail our brother ?   He hath gone
To sit down with the prophets by the clear
And crystal waters ; he hath gone to list
Isaiah's harp and David's, and to walk
With Enoch, and Elijah, and the host
Of the just men made perfect.   He shall bow
At Gabriel's hallelujah, and unfold
The scroll of the Apocalypse with John,
And talk of Christ with Mary, and go back
To the last supper, and the garden prayer
With the beloved disciple.   He shall hear
The story of the Incarnation told
By Simeon, and the Triune mystery
Burning upon the fervent lips of Paul.
He shall have wings of glory, and shall soar

To the remoter firmaments, and read
The order and the harmony of stars;
And, in the might of knowledge, he shall bow,
In the deep pauses of archangel harps,
And, humble as the Seraphim, shall cry—
Who, by his searching, finds thee out, O God!

There shall he meet his children who have gone
Before him, and as other years roll on,
And his loved flock go up to him, his hand
Again shall lead them gently to the Lamb,
And bring them to the living waters there.

Is it so good to die! and shall we mourn
That he is taken early to his rest?
Tell me! oh mourner for the man of God!
Shall we bewail our brother—that he died?

IDLENESS.

"Idleness is sweet and sacred."
—WALTER SAVAGE LANDOR.

"When you have found a day to be idle, be idle for a day.
When you have met with three cups to drink, drink your three cups."
—CHINESE POET.

THE rain is playing its soft pleasant tune
Fitfully on the skylight, and the shade
Of the fast-flying clouds across my book
Passes with delicate change. My merry fire
Sings cheerfully to itself; my musing cat
Purrs as she wakes from her unquiet sleep,
And looks into my face as if she felt,
Like me, the gentle influence of the rain.
Here have I sat since morn, reading sometimes,

And sometimes listening to the faster fall
Of the large drops, or rising with the stir
Of an unbidden thought, have walk'd awhile,
With the slow steps of indolence, my room,
And then sat down composedly again
To my quaint book of olden poetry.

It is a kind of idleness, I know;
And I am said to be an idle man—
And it is very true.   I love to go
Out in the pleasant sun, and let my eye
Rest on the human faces that pass by,
Each with its gay or busy interest :
And then I muse upon their lot, and read
Many a lesson in their changeful cast,
And so grow kind of heart, as if the sight
Of human beings were humanity.
And I am better after it, and go
More gratefully to my rest, and feel a love
Stirring my heart to every living thing ;
And my low prayer has more humility,
And I sink lighter to my dreams—and this,
'Tis very true, is only idleness !

I love to go and mingle with the young
In the gay festal room—when every heart
Is beating faster than the merry tune,
And their blue eyes are restless, and the lips
Parted with eager joy, and their round cheeks
Flush'd with the beautiful motion of the dance.
And I can look upon such things, and go
Back to my solitude, and dream bright dreams
For their fast coming years, and speak of them
Earnestly in my prayer, till I am glad
With a benevolent joy—and this, I know,
To the world's eye is only idleness !

And when the clouds pass suddenly away,
And the blue sky is like a newer world,
And the sweet-growing things—forest and flower,
Humble and beautiful alike—are all
Breathing up odours to the very heaven—
Or when the frost has yielded to the sun
In the rich autumn, and the filmy mist
Lies like a silver lining on the sky,
And the clear air exhilarates, and life
Simply, is luxury—and when the hush
Of twilight, like a gentle sleep, steals on,
And the birds settle to their nests, and stars
Spring in the upper sky, and there is not
A sound that is not low and musical—
At all these pleasant seasons I go out
With my first impulse guiding me, and take
Wood-path or stream, or slope by hill or vale,
And in my recklessness of heart, stray on,
Glad with the birds, and silent with the leaves,
And happy with the fair and blessed world—
And this, 'tis true, is only idleness !

And I should love to go up to the sky,
And course the heavens, like stars, and float away
Upon the gliding clouds that have no stay
In their swift journey—and 'twould be a joy
To walk the chambers of the deep, and tread
The pearls of its untrodden floor, and know
The tribes of the unfathomable depths —
Dwellers beneath the pressure of a sea !
And I should love to issue with the wind
On a strong errand, and o'ersweep the earth
With its broad continents and islands green,
Like to the passing of a spirit on !—
And this, 'tis true, were only idleness !

JANUARY 1, 1828.

FLEETLY hath pass'd the year. The seasons came
Duly as they are wont—the gentle Spring,
And the delicious Summer, and the cool,
Rich Autumn, with the nodding of the grain,
And Winter, like an old and hoary man,
Frosty and stiff—and so are chronicled.
We have read gladness in the new green leaf,
And in the first blown violets; we have drunk
Cool water from the rock, and in the shade
Sunk to the noon-tide slumber ;—we have pluck'd
The mellow fruitage of the bending tree,
And girded to our pleasant wanderings
When the cool wind came freshly from the hills ;
And when the tinting of the Autumn leaves
Had faded from its glory, we have sat
By the good fires of Winter, and rejoiced
Over the fulness of the gather'd sheaf.
" God hath been very good ! "   'Tis He whose hand
Moulded the sunny hills, and hollow'd out
The shelter of the valleys, and doth keep
The fountains in their secret places cool ;
And it is He who leadeth up the sun,
And ordereth the starry influences,
And tempereth the keenness of the frost—
And therefore, in the plenty of the feast,
And in the lifting of the cup, let HIM
Have praise for the well-completed year.

ON A PICTURE OF A GIRL LEADING HER BLIND MOTHER THROUGH THE WOOD.

THE green leaves as we pass
    Lay their light fingers on thee unaware,
And by thy side the hazels cluster fair,
    And the low forest-grass
Grows green and silken where the wood-paths wind—
Alas! for thee, sweet mother! thou art blind!

    And nature is all bright;
And the faint grey and crimson of the dawn,
Like folded curtains from the day are drawn;
    And evening's purple light
Quivers in tremulous softness on the sky—
Alas! sweet mother! for thy clouded eye!

    The moon's new silver shell
Trembles above thee, and the stars float up,
In the blue air, and the rich tulip's cup
    Is pencill'd passing well,
And the swift birds on glorious pinions flee—
Alas! sweet mother! that thou canst not see!

    And the kind looks of friends
Peruse the sad expression in thy face,
And the child stops amid his bounding race,
    And the tall stripling bends
Low to thine ear with duty unforgot—
Alas! sweet mother! that thou seest them not!

    But thou canst *hear!* and love
May richly on a human tone be pour'd,
And the least cadence of a whisper'd word
    A daughter's love may prove—

And while I speak thou knowest if I smile,
Albeit thou canst not see my face the while !

    Yes, thou canst hear ! and He
Who on thy sightless eye its darkness hung,
To the attentive ear, like harps, hath strung
    Heaven and earth and sea !
And 'tis a lesson in our hearts to know—
With but one sense the soul may overflow.

JANUARY 1, 1829.

WINTER is come again. The sweet south-west
Is a forgotten wind, and the strong earth
Has laid aside its mantle to be bound
By the frost fetter. There is not a sound,
Save of the skater's heel : and there is laid
An icy finger on the lip of streams,
And the clear icicle hangs cold and still,
And the snow-fall is noiseless as a thought.
Spring has a rushing sound, and Summer sends
Many sweet voices with its odours out,
And Autumn rustleth its decaying robe
With a complaining whisper. Winter's dumb !
God made his ministry a silent one,
And He has given him a foot of steel
And an unlovely aspect, and a breath
Sharp to the senses—and we know that He
Tempereth well, and hath a meaning hid
Under the shadow of His hand. Look up ;
And it shall be interpreted—Your home
Hath a temptation now ! There is no voice
Of waters with beguiling for your ear,
And the cool forest and the meadows green

Witch not your feet away; and in the dells
There are no violets, and upon the hills
There are no sunny places to lie down.
You must go in, and by your cheerful fire
Wait for the offices of love, and hear
Accents of human tenderness, and feast
Your eye upon the beauty of the young.
It is a season for the quiet thought,
And the still reckoning with thyself.   The year
Gives back the spirits of its dead, and time
Whispers the history of its vanish'd hours;
And the heart, calling its affections up,
Counteth its wasted ingots.   Life stands still
And settles like a fountain, and the eye
Sees clearly through its depths, and noteth all
That stirr'd its troubled waters.   It is well
That Winter with the dying year should come !

PSYCHE,

Before the Tribunal of Venus.

LIFT up thine eyes, sweet Psyche ! What is she,
That those soft fringes timidly should fall
Before her, and thy spiritual brow
Be dark, as if her presence were a cloud ?
A loftier gift is thine than she can give—
That queen of beauty.   She may mould the brow
To perfectness, and give unto the form
A beautiful proportion; she may stain
The eye with a celestial blue—the cheek
With carmine of the sunset; she may breathe
Grace into every motion, like the play
Of the least visible tissue of a cloud;

She may give all that is within her own
Bright cestus—and one silent look of thine,
Like stronger magic, will outcharm it all.

Ay, for the soul is better than its frame,
The spirit than its temple.   What's the brow,
Or the eye's lustre, or the step of air,
Or colour, but the beautiful links that chain
The mind from its rare element ?   There lies
A talisman in intellect which yields
Celestial music, when the master hand
Touches it cunningly.   It sleeps beneath
The outward semblance, and to common sight
Is an invisible and hidden thing ;
But when the lip is faded, and the cheek
Robb'd of its daintiness, and when the form
Witches the sense no more, and human love
Falters in its idolatry, this spell
Will hold its strength unbroken, and go on
Stealing anew the affections.

                         Marvel not
That Love leans sadly on his bended bow.
He hath found out the loveliness of mind,
And he is spoilt for beauty.   So 'twill be
Ever—the glory of the human form
Is but a perishing thing, and Love will droop
When its brief grace hath faded ; but the mind
Perisheth not, and when the outward charm
Hath had its brief existence, it awakes,
And is the lovelier that it slept so long—
Like wells that by the wasting of their flow
Have had their deeper fountains broken up.

T

ON SEEING A BEAUTIFUL BOY AT PLAY.

Down the green slope he bounded.   Raven curls
From his white shoulders by the winds were swept,
And the clear colour of his sunny cheek
Was bright with motion.   Through his open lips
Shone visibly a delicate line of pearl,
Like a white vein within a rosy shell,
And his dark eye's clear brilliance, as it lay
Beneath his lashes, like a drop of dew
Hid in the moss, stole out as covertly
As starlight from the edging of a cloud.
I never saw a boy so beautiful.
His step was like the stooping of a bird,
And his limbs melted into grace like things
Shaped by the wind of summer.   He was like
A painter's conception—such an one
As he would have of Ganymede, and weep
Upon his pallet that he could not win
The vision to his easel.   Who could paint
The young and shadowless spirit ?   Who could chain
The visible gladness of a heart that lives,
Like a glad fountain, in the eye of light,
With an unbreathing pencil ?   Nature's gift
Has nothing that is like it.   Sun and stream,
And the new leaves of June, and the young lark
That flees away into the depths of heaven,
Lost in his own wild music, and the breath
Of springtime, and the summer eve, and noon
In the cool autumn, are like fingers swept
Over sweet-toned affections—but the joy
That enters to the spirit of a child
Is deep as his young heart : his very breath,
The simple sense of being, is enough

To ravish him, and like a thrilling touch
He feels each moment of his life go by.

Beautiful, beautiful childhood! with a joy
That like a robe is palpable, and flung
Out by your every motion! delicate bud
Of the immortal flower that will unfold
And come to its maturity in heaven!
I weep your earthly glory. 'Tis a light
Lent to the new-born spirit, that goes out
With the first idle wind. It is the leaf
Fresh flung upon the river, that will dance
Upon the wave that stealeth out its life,
Then sink of its own heaviness. The face
Of the delightful earth will to your eye
Grow dim; the fragrance of the many flowers
Be noticed not, and the beguiling voice
Of nature in her gentleness will be
To manhood's senseless ear inaudible.
I sigh to look upon thy face, young boy!

HERO.

Claudio. Know you any, Hero?
Hero. None, my lord!
Much Ado about Nothing.

GENTLE and modest Hero! I can see
Her delicate figure, and her soft blue eye,
Like a warm vision—lovely as she stood,
Veil'd in the presence of Claudio.
Modesty bows her head, and that young heart
That would endure all suffering for the love
It hideth, is as tremulous as the leaf
Forsaken of the Summer. She hath flung

Her all upon the venture of her vow,
And in her trust leans meekly, like a flower
By the still river tempted from its stem,
And on its bosom floating.

                                    Once again
I see her, and she standeth in her pride,
With her soft eye enkindled, and her lip
Curled with its sweet resentment, like a line
Of lifeless coral.   She hath heard the voice
That was her music utter it, and still
To her affection faithful, she hath turn'd
And question'd, in her innocent unbelief,
" Is my lord well, that he should speak so wide ? "
How did they look upon that open brow,
And not read purity ?   Alas for truth !
It hath so many counterfeits.   The words,
That to a child were written legibly,
Are by the wise mistaken, and when light
Hath made the brow transparent, and the face
Is like an angel's—virtue is so fair—
They read it like an over-blotted leaf,
And break the heart that wrote it.

SPIRIT-WHISPERS.

*(Spirit-whisper in the poet's ear—*MORNING.*)*

WAKE ! poet, wake !—the morn has burst
   Through gates of stars and dew,
And, wing'd by prayer since evening nursed,
Has fled to kiss the steeples first,
   And now stoops low to you !
Oh, poet of the loving eye,
For you is dress'd this morning sky !

(Second whisper—NOON.)

Oh, poet of the pen enchanted !
   A lady sits beneath a tree !
At last the flood for which she panted—
The wild words for her anguish wanted,
   Have gush'd in song from thee !
Her dark curls sweep her knees to pray :—
" God bless the poet far away ! "

(Third whisper—MIDNIGHT.)

King of the heart's deep mysteries !
   Your words have wings like lightning wove !
This hour, o'er hills and distant seas,
They fly like flower-seeds on the breeze,
   And sow the world with love !
King of a realm without a throne,
Ruled by resistless tears alone !

POEM

Delivered at Brown University, Sept. 6, 1831.

IF, in the eyes that rest upon me now,
I see the light of an immortal fire—
If in the awe of concentrated thought,
The solemn presence of a multitude
Breathing together, the instinctive mind
Acknowledges aright a type of God—
Then is the ruling spirit of this hour
Compell'd from Heaven ; and if the soaring minds
Usher'd this day upon an untried flight
Stoop not their courses, we are met to cheer
Spirits of light sprung freshly on their way.

But, what a mystery—this erring mind ?
It wakes within a frame of various powers
A stranger in a new and wondrous world.
It brings an instinct from some other sphere,
For its fine senses are familiar all,
And, with the unconscious habit of a dream,
It calls, and they obey.   The priceless sight
Springs to its curious organ, and the ear
Learns strangely to detect th' articulate air
In its unseen divisions, and the tongue
Gets its miraculous lesson with the rest,
And in the midst of an obedient throng
Of well-trained ministers, the mind goes forth
To search the secrets of a new-found home.

Its infancy is full of hope and joy.
Knowledge is sweet, and Nature is a nurse
Gentle and holy ; and the light and air
And all things common, warm it like the sun,
And ripen the eternal seed within.
And so its youth glides on ; and still it seems
A heavenward spirit, straying oftentimes,
But never widely ; and if death might come
And ravish it from earth, as it is now,
We could almost believe that it would mount,
Spotless and radiant, from the very grave.
But manhood comes, and in its bosom sits
Another spirit.   Stranger as it seems,
It is familiar there, for it has grown
In the unsearch'd recesses all unseen,—
Or if its shadow darken'd the bright doors,
'Twas smiled upon and gently driven in ;
And as the spider and the honey-bee
Feed on the same bright flowers, this mocking soul
Fed with its purer brother, and grew strong,

Till now, in semblance of the soul itself,
With its own mien and sceptre, and a voice
Sweet as an angel's and as full of power,
It sits, a bold usurper on the throne.
What is its nature? 'Tis a child of clay,
And born of human passions. In its train
Follow all things unholy—Love of Gold,
Ambition, Pleasure, Pride of place or name,
All that we worship for itself alone,
All that we may not carry through the grave.
We have made idols of these perishing things
Till they have grown time-honour'd on their shrines,
And all men bow to them. Yet what *are* they?
What is AMBITION? 'Tis a glorious cheat!
Angels of light walk not so dazzlingly
The sapphire walls of Heaven. The unsearch'd mine
Hath not such gems. Earth's constellated thrones
Have not such pomp of purple and of gold.
It hath no features. In its face is set
A mirror, and the gazer sees his own.
It looks a God, but it is like *himself!*
It hath a mien majestical, and smiles
Bewilderingly sweet—but how like *him!*
It follows not with fortune. It is seen
Rarely or never in the rich man's hall.
It seeks the chamber of a gifted boy,
And lifts his humble window, and comes in.
The narrow walls expand, and spread away
Into a kingly palace, and the roof
Lifts to the sky, and unseen fingers work
The ceilings with rich blazonry, and write
His name in burning letters over all.
And ever, as he shuts his 'wilder'd eyes,
The phantom comes and lays upon his lids
A spell that murders sleep, and in his ear

Whispers a deathless word, and on his brain
Breathes a fierce thirst no water will allay.
He is its slave henceforth !   His days are spent
In chaining down his heart, and watching where
To rise by human weaknesses.   His nights
Bring him no rest in all their blessed hours.
His kindred are forgotten or estranged.
Unhealthful fires burn constant in his eye,
His lip grows restless, and its smile is curl'd
Half into scorn—till the bright, fiery boy,
That was a daily blessing but to see,
His spirit was so bird-like and so pure,
Is frozen, in the very flush of youth,
Into a cold, care-fretted, heartless *man !*

And what is its reward ?   At best, a name !
Praise—when the ear has grown too dull to hear,
Gold—when the senses it should please are dead ;
Wreaths—when the hair they cover has grown grey ;
Fame—when the heart it should have thrill'd is numb,
All things but *love*—when love is all we want ;
And close behind comes Death, and ere we know
That ev'n these unavailing gifts are ours,
He sends us, stripp'd and naked, to the grave.

Is it *its own* reward ?   Reply to it,
Every aspiring heart within these walls
Summon the shadows of those bitter hours
Wasted in brooding or neglect !   Recall
The burning tears wrung from a throbbing brain
By a proud effort foil'd ; and after all
These agonies are number'd, rack your heart
Back to its own self-nurtured wretchedness.
And when the pangs are crowded into one
Of all life's scorpion-stings, and Death itself
Is sent or stay'd, as it would bless or curse,

Tell me if *self-misgiving* torture not
Unutterably more !

   Yet this is all !
The world has no such glorious phantom else.
The spirit that could slave itself to *Gold*
Hath never drunk of knowledge at the well.
And *Pleasure*, if the senses would expand
And multiply with using, might delude
The flesh-imprison'd fancy—but not long.
And earthly *Love*—if measured, is too tame—
And if it drink, as in proud hearts it will,
At the deep springs of life, is but a cloud
Brooding with nameless sorrow on the soul—
A sadness—a sick-heartedness—a tear !

 And these are the high idols of this world !
Retreating shadows caught but at the grave—
Mocking delusions, changing at the touch—
Of one false spirit the false children all.
And yet, what godlike gifts neglected lie
Wasting and marr'd in the forgotten soul !
The finest workmanship of God is there.
'Tis fleeter than the wings of light and wind ;
'Tis subtler than the rarest shape of air ;
Fire and wind and water do its will ;
Earth hath no secret from its delicate eye ;
The air no alchymy it solveth not ;
The star-writ heavens are read and understood,
And every sparry mineral hath a name,
And truth is recognised, and beauty felt,
And God's own image stamp'd upon its brow.

 How is it so forgotten ? *Will* it live
When the great firmament is roll'd away ?
Hath it a voice for ever audible,

" I am eternal ! "   *Can* it overcome
This mocking passion-fiend, and even here
Live like a seraph upon truth and light ?

How can we ever be the slaves we are,
With a sweet angel sitting in our breasts !
How can we creep so lowly, when our wings
Tremble and plead for freedom !   Look at him
Who reads aright the image on his soul,
And gives it nurture like a child of light.
His life is calm and blessed, for his peace,
Like a rich pearl beyond the diver's ken,
Lies deep in his own bosom.   He is pure,
For the soul's errands are not done with men.
His senses are subdued and serve the soul.
He feels no void, for every faculty
Is used, and the fine balance of desire
Is perfect, and strains evenly, and on.
Content dwells with him, for his mind is fed,
And Temperance has driven out unrest.
He heaps no gold.   It cannot buy him more
Of anything he needs.   The air of heaven
Visits no freshlier the rich man's brow ;
He has his portion of each silver star
Sent to his eye so freely, and the light
Of the blest sun pours on his book so clear
As on the golden missal of a king.
The spicy flowers are free to him ; the sward,
And tender moss, and matted forest leaves
Are as elastic to his weary feet ;
The pictures in the fountains, and beneath
The spreading trees, fine pencillings of light,
Stay while he gazes on them ; the bright birds
Know not that he is poor ; and as he comes
From his low roof at morn, up goes the lark

Mounting and singing to the gate of Heaven,
And merrily away the little brook
Trips with its feet of silver, and a voice,
Almost articulate, of perfect joy.
Air to his forehead, water to his lips,
Heat to his blood, come just as faithfully,
And his own faculties as freely play.
Love fills his voice with music, and the tear
Springs at as light a bidding to his eye ;
And his free limbs obey him, and his sight
Flies on its wondrous errands everywhere.

What does he need ?   Next to the works of God
His friends are the rapt sages of old time ;
And they impart their wisdom to his soul
In lavish fulness, when and where he will.
He sits in his mean dwelling and communes
With Socrates and Plato, and the shades
Of all great men and holy, and the words
Written in fire by Milton, and the King
Of Israel, and the troop of glorious bards,
Ravish and steal his soul up to the sky—
And what is it to him, if these come in
And visit him, that at his humble door
There are no pillars with rich capitals
And walls of curious workmanship within ?

I stand here in Wisdom's sacred stole.
My lips have not been touch'd with holy fire.
An humbler office than a counsellor
Of human duties, and an humbler place,
Would better grace my knowledge and my years.
I would not seem presuming.   Yet have I
Mingled a little in this earnest world,
And staked upon its chances, and have learn'd
Truths that I never gather'd from my books.

And though the lessons they have taught me seem
Things of the wayside to the practised *man,*
It is a wisdom by much wandering learn'd ;
And if but one young spirit bend its wing
More in the eye of Heaven, because it knew
The erring courses that bewilder'd mine,
I have not suffer'd nor shall teach in vain.

It is a lesson oftener learn'd than loved—
All knowledge is not nourishment. The mind
May pine upon its food. In reckless thirst
The scholar sometimes kneels beside the stream
Polluted by the lepers of the mind.
The sceptic, with his doubts of all things good
And faith in all things evil, has been there ;
And, as the stream was mingled, he has strown
The shore with all bright flowers to tempt the eye,
And sloped the banks down gently for the feet ;
And Genius, like a fallen child of light,
Has fill'd the place with magic, and compell'd
Most beautiful creations into forms
And images of license, and they come
And tempt you with bewildering grace to kneel
And drink of the wild waters ; and behind
Stand the strong Passions, pleading to go in ;
And the approving world looks silent on ;
Till the pleased mind conspires against itself,
And finds a subtle reason why 'tis good.
We are deceived, though, even as we drink,
We taste the evil. In his sweetest tone
The lying Tempter whispers in our ear,
" Though it may stain, 'twill *strengthen* your proud wings ; "
And in the wild ambition of the soul
We drink anew, and dream like Lucifer
To mount upon our daring draught to Heaven.

I need not follow the similitude.
Truth is *vitality*, and if the mind
Be fed on poison, it *must* lose its power.
The vision that for ever strains to err,
Soon finds its task a habit; and the taste
That will own nothing true or beautiful
Soon finds the world distorted as itself;
And the loose mind, that feeds an appetite
For the enticements of licentious thought,
Contracts a leprosy that oversteals
Its senses, like a palsy, chill, and fast.

Another lesson with my manhood came.
I have unlearn'd contempt. It is the sin
That is engender'd earliest in the soul,
And doth beset it like a poison-worm,
Feeding on all its beauty. As it steals
Into the bosom, you may see the light
Of the clear, heavenly eye grew cold and dim,
And the fine, upright glory of the brow
Cloud with mistrust, and the unfetter'd lip,
That was as free and changeful as the wind—
Even in sadness redolent of love—
Curl'd with the iciness of a constant scorn.
It eats into the mind till it pollutes
All its pure fountains. Feeling, reason, taste,
Breathe of its chill corruption. Every sense
That could convey a pleasure is benumb'd,
And the bright human being, that was made
Full of all warm affections, and with power
To look through all things lovely up to God,
Is changed into a cold and doubting fiend,
With but one use for reason—*to despise !*

Oh, if there is one law above the rest
Written in reason—if there is a word

That I could trace as with a pen of fire
Upon the unsunn'd temper of a child—
If there is any thing that keeps the mind
Open to angel visits, and repels
The ministry of ill—'tis human love !
God has made nothing worthy of contempt.
The smallest pebble in the well of truth
Has its peculiar meaning, and will stand
When men's best monuments have pass'd away.
The law of heaven is *love ;* and though its name
Has been usurped by passion, and profaned
To its unholy uses through all time,
Still, the eternal principle is pure ;
And in these deep affections that we feel
Omnipotent within us, we but see
The lavish measure in which love is given ;
And in the yearning tenderness of a child
For every bird that sings above his head,
And every creature feeding on the hills,
And every tree, and flower, and running brook,
We see how every thing was *made to love.*
And how they err, who, in a world like this,
Find anything to hate but human pride !

Oh, if we are not bitterly deceived—
If this familiar spirit that communes
With yours this hour—that has the power to search
All things but its own compass—*is* a spark
Struck from the burning essence of its God—
If, as we dream, in every radiant star
We see a shining gate through which the soul,
In its degrees of being, will ascend—
If, when these weary organs drop away,
We shall forget their uses, and commune
With angels and each other, as the stars

Mingle their light, in silence and in love—
What is this fleshly fetter of a day
That we should bind it with immortal flowers!
How do we ever gaze upon the sky,
And watch the lark soar up till he is lost,
And turn to our poor perishing dreams away,
Without one tear for our imprison'd wings!

UPON THE PORTRAIT OF THE HON. MRS. STANHOPE.

WHAT dost thou hear?
Has the hymn of a fairy reach'd thine ear?
Dost thou list the praise of thy beauty, sung
By the amorous leaves thou art lost among?
Is the cluster of buds and roses there,
Of the presence of lips more bright, aware?
And have they a voice, as minstrels say,
For all things dewy and fair as they?

What dost thou see?
Has a sky-bound angel stooped to thee?
Doth some loving zephyr, with wings of light,
Hover revealed in thy mortal sight?
Has a ray of a star, that should sleep by day,
Stole back with the sun, in thine eyes to play?
Do light and air, as the minstrel sings,
Yearn to the fairest of mortal things?

Ay—gaze and listen!
On thy Phidian brow the bright gems glisten,
But the gnomes that wrought these diamonds fine,
Knew not their bed in the Indian mine,

As the spirits of love in earth and air
Know every charm in a form so fair.
Thou wast never alone, oh lovely one !
By dewy morn or by setting sun.

Thou hast felt a thrill, thou know'st not why,
From the summer mind, from the golden sky—
The slightest leaf, the meanest flower,
Has touched thy heart in some lonely hour—
Though the fondest friend had farthest flown,
Thou hadst not been in that hour alone !

Oh, the life that stirs in the panting rose—
The vital breath in each breeze that blows—
The far sent ray of the arrowy light—
Perfume and Music, by day and night—
I have sometimes thought they come and go,
With a spirit's power to see and know,
And tremble with love in their vainless sphere,
     And whisper low,
When forms of the beauty of heaven are near.

THE END.